WHAT WENT
WRONG
WITH
BREXIT

WHAT WENT

AND WHAT

WRONG

WE CAN DO

WITH

ABOUT IT

BREXIT

PETER FOSTER

CANONGATE

First published in Great Britain in 2023 by Canongate Books Ltd,
14 High Street, Edinburgh EH1 1TE

canongate.co.uk

2

British Library Cataloguing-in-Publication Data
A catalogue record for this book is available on
request from the British Library

ISBN 978 1 80530 125 7

Typeset in Bembo by Palimpsest Book Production Ltd,
Falkirk, Stirlingshire

Printed and bound in Great Britain by Clays Ltd, Elcograf S.p.A.

MIX
Paper from
responsible sources
FSC® C018072

For Clare
and
Billy, Lila, Scarlett

Contents

Introduction

The Original Sin

A few weeks before the Brexit referendum of June 2016 I found myself sitting on an EasyJet flight en route to Vienna for an article about the rise of populist politics in Europe. Sitting next to me were two guys from London's East End, one in his mid-20s, the other in his early 50s, who were going to the Austrian capital to erect digital advertising signage for a motor-sport event. They were a perfect example of the economic benefits of EU membership: flying visa-free to deliver goods and services in a foreign country on a low-cost airline made possible by the EU's single market for aviation. Since the vote was looming, the conversation inevitably fell to discussing the rights and wrongs of Brexit. The younger man was instinctively for Remain but hadn't bothered to find out much about it and said he probably wasn't going to vote at all; but his older colleague was emphatically for Leave. 'We just got to get out,' he said. I expressed surprise to hear that from him. Wouldn't Brexit make it harder to conduct the business that was currently paying his wages? 'Maybe, but I think Britain will be fine. And even if it did, I still don't care,' he said. 'We just got to go. We need to be free from Brussels telling us what to do all the time and all that red tape.'

It is true that for many people Brexit wasn't about raw economics, but in some sense it had to be about a brighter future for Britain. No one votes for a darker future, after all. Some Brexiters, like that freely moving worker on the flight to Vienna, said that they accepted that leaving the EU may cause economic damage, but still held the belief that the UK would be 'better off out'. That's because the overarching offer that was made to British voters in 2016 by the Brexit campaign was that outside the EU, the UK would be happier, healthier and freer. By reducing uncontrolled immigration after two decades of flat wages and opening up the prospects of global trade to faster-growing markets on the other side of the world, Brexiters promised that quitting Europe would enable the UK to float free of its Continental 'ball-and-chain'. In the phrase of the former Conservative and UK Independence Party MP Douglas Carswell, the UK would no longer be 'shackled to the corpse' of Europe. The implication was that EU membership had emasculated Britain and that, via Brexit, the virility of the nation could be restored. As the victorious UKIP leader Nigel Farage put it: 'Let June 23rd go down in our history as our Independence Day!'

While the vote to leave had proximate causes, like the 2015 migrant crisis in which over a million refugees arrived in Europe as they fled civil war in Syria, the foundations were laid over many decades. From the start, the UK had always been instinctively nervous of the supranational elements of European integration, not engaging with the founding Treaty of Rome in 1957, but preferring to focus on the Commonwealth and the dream of a global economic system with sterling at its heart. These misgivings never went away, even after the UK joined the European club in 1973, and they deepened still further following the 1992 Maastricht Treaty. By the time Boris Johnson was a correspondent in Brussels for the *Daily Telegraph* in the early 1990s, sending back rollicking stories about bendy bananas, the idea of the EU as a sovereignty-sapping federal superstate was constantly being drip-fed into British popular thinking by a jingoistic tabloid media. An opportunity was never missed to fuel ideas of British exceptionalism based on the *Dad's Army* school of international affairs: plucky Britain standing alone in the face of overbearing attempts to unify Europe. Johnson was explicit about this during the 2016 referendum campaign: 'Napoleon, Hitler, various people tried this out, and it ends tragically,' he said. 'The EU is an attempt to do this by different methods.'

This narrative was so all-pervasive that even those who voted to remain often did so for negative rather than positive reasons – clinging to the safety of the status quo rather than actively embracing the idea that Britain could have a positive role in shaping the wider European neighbourhood. Perhaps this was not surprising, since over the decades very few British politicians, Labour or Tory, had ever dared to make a positive case for the benefits of EU membership, at least in public. Those benefits were economic, but also cultural and geopolitical as the EU became the foundation for a peaceful post-war Europe. Brexiters, on the other hand, believed they were voting for a radical and exciting transformation, reasserting an individual national identity by leaving the European collective without economic or cultural costs. Voters like to 'have their cake and eat it as much as their politicians. It is why, in the end, the Leave side won the vote.

Seven years after the vote to leave the EU, it is becoming clearer by the day that that promised future turns out not to exist. Brexit was first and foremost a political project to 'take back control' of law-making and borders in order to remake Britain as a globally influential actor. But having repatriated powers from Brussels, Brexit has instead delivered political instability at home and embarrassment abroad, surprisingly high levels of immigration, weak borders and poor trade performance, corrosive levels of business uncertainty and – ironically – all with limited scrutiny from the newly sovereign UK parliament. The economics of Brexit is rapidly catching up with the politics of Brexit, and the two cannot remain divorced for ever.

This book is about why that is the case and, much more importantly, about what we can do to fix the mess. Because more than seven years after the vote to leave, it is time to look forward not back. There is little mileage in relitigating the history of Brexit – as the saying goes, 'we are where we are' – but that does not mean accepting that the UK has to remain in its current state of Brexit purgatory. Far from 'taking back control', the UK has in fact been left in a state of limbo by Brexit. Moving on means that those, like Boris Johnson or Nigel Farage, who were allowed to define Brexit in its current form, should not be granted a monopoly of wisdom about what Brexit might mean in the future. Talk of 'selling out' or 'betraying' Brexit – by which they mean the *Dad's Army* version of Brexit – is an attempt to close down a debate about the scope of the UK's relations with Europe. This is a debate the UK urgently needs to have. The last seven years have poisoned British politics, unsettled the foundations of Britain's unwritten constitution, curtailed trade, rattled investors and tarnished the UK's reputation abroad as a pragmatic power that can be trusted. By the end of 2022, two years after the UK–EU post-Brexit trade deal came into force, the UK's exports (excluding precious metals) were more than 9 per cent below the 2019 pre-pandemic average, putting the UK right at the bottom of the G7 pack. The Resolution Foundation think tank described the UK trade performance since Brexit as 'a disaster'.

The good news is that space is now emerging for a rethink. Polls clearly show that a growing proportion of the public are coming to see that much of what they were told about the 'benefits of Brexit' have turned out to be untrue. The shift in the public mood has been matched on the diplomatic front by Prime Minister Rishi Sunak's politically astute Windsor Framework to resolve the stand-off with Brussels over Northern Ireland. This has re-opened the door to discussion with Europe on a range of other topics, from energy security to scientific collaboration at both the EU and bilateral levels. The coming general election could provide a further political inflection point. The Northern Ireland Assembly will hold its first consent vote in 2024 on whether to continue to accept the newly refurbished post-Brexit trading arrangements. And after 2025, the low-ambition EU–UK trade deal agreed by the former prime minister Boris Johnson is also up for review, giving the UK a chance to improve terms with the economic bloc that takes nearly half the UK's trade. All these provide potential footholds to rebuild broken relationships, but only if there is sufficiently brave political leadership to shift the Brexit debate away from toxic notions of 'betrayal' and back onto the economic well-being of the nation.

But any fruitful discussion about the future must be predicated on a clearer understanding of why the current version of Brexit is failing – and why that is an entirely predictable function of its design, not an unexpected failure of execution. The negative economic consequences of Brexit, far from being the result of some brave gamble gone wrong, were completely foreseeable. In fact, they were foreseen, including by several of those responsible for delivering the current settlement, like Boris Johnson, David Frost and Liz Truss, who were all at different points admirably clear about the costs of leaving the EU, until it suited them politically to say otherwise. With EU integration having progressed so far via the construction of the EU single market, the economic benefits of membership – plugging British manufacturers and professional service providers directly into a vast market of consumers – very clearly outweigh the costs. The UK can bemoan this from the sidelines, if it wants, but it cannot deny the reality. It's why leading Eurosceptic leaders like Marine Le Pen in France or Matteo Salvini in Italy quickly gave up talking about 'Frexit' or 'Italexit' after 2016. They understood the destruction of value that would cause. The case for Brexit was that the UK, being a large and innovative economy outside the Eurozone, was in some way exceptional. But it wasn't. And it isn't.

The dreaded 'Brussels red tape' that was so enthusiastically mocked by the Eurosceptic press, far from choking British industry, on balance enabled business to trade freely with the advanced economies on our doorstep. True, EU regulation wasn't always perfectly suited to the UK economy because it yoked together 27 other economies, but it provided friction-free access to a market of 450 million people. Brexit turned Brussels 'red tape' into British 'red, white and blue tape', and lots of it. Joining the EU single market – what Carswell called 'this poverty-producing club' – in truth made the British economy more competitive, not less so. It reduced costs and exposed UK industry to the advanced competitors on its doorstep, which in turn drove innovation, investment and productivity. The free movement of people caused social dislocation at home, but it also opened massive opportunities abroad for the UK to sell the services – professional and cultural – at which our economy excelled. Similarly, EU membership did not constrain our ability to trade around the world. On the contrary, it gave the UK access to nearly 70 international trade agreements. The Netherlands and Germany were better at seizing the opportunities these deals created, it is true, but Britain did not need to leave the EU to boost its overseas trade. Brexiters bragged about the prospects for 'global Britain' without acknowledging they were already part of the world's biggest trading bloc, whose rules made the regulatory weather for businesses all over the planet.

As a result, Brexit has thus far damaged the prospects for UK trade and investment, not improved them. The promised raft of post-Brexit free trade agreements with other countries hasn't turned up. And even if all those promised deals were struck – and we're still waiting for major deals, including with the USA – they're economically insignificant when set against the costs of Brexit, according to the Government's own estimates. The cost of building back barriers between the UK and the single market full of wealthy consumers on its doorstep is about 20 times the value of UK trade deals, in a best-case scenario. From a purely business perspective, Brexit is a trade-off that no CEO in their right mind would ever have made. The promise of a deregulatory nirvana to offset the costs of building back borders with our biggest trade partner also hasn't materialised. This is because, however frantically Brexit-believers exhort British companies to embrace deregulation, for much of industry and the public this doesn't make sense. True, conforming to regulation creates cost for business, but that same red tape also creates certainty, builds consumer confidence and a 'level playing field' on which to trade across borders.

So what price freedom? Trade with the EU is now more expensive than it was before Brexit thanks to new bureaucratic barriers. These are likely to increase, not diminish, over time as EU countries continue to integrate the physical, financial and regulatory frameworks that undergird their economies. In simple terms, Brexit has made the UK less competitive, less open and less productive than it otherwise would have been. The UK is falling behind its competitors. UK trade performance has been much weaker than the G7 average since the Brexit trade deal came into force. UK business investment, which creates the next generation of better-paying jobs, has flatlined since 2016. Researchers at the London School of Economics (LSE) calculated that by the end of 2021, Brexit had already cost UK households a total of £5.8 billion in higher food bills. Over the next decade the Resolution Foundation think tank, which focuses on the lives of those on lower and middle incomes, says we can expect the wages of UK workers to fall by £470 per worker a year – thanks to Brexit.

The pain of the last seven years is not solely economic. Arguably even more damaging has been the political fallout caused by post-Brexit governments trying to reconcile what they hoped to be true before Brexit with the reality of life outside the EU. The process of trying to make Brexit work, often in the face of all the evidence, has had deeply corrosive secondary effects. These have undermined the foundations of the British state and constitution, straining relationships between the government and parliament; politicians and judges; ministers and civil servants; and the UK government and the devolved administrations in Scotland, Wales and, especially, Northern Ireland, where Brexit issues have caused the collapse of the devolved government. The result is that dishonesty over the consequences of Brexit has become a chronic condition in British politics.

That urgently needs to change. 'Take Back Control' was a brilliant political slogan. It enabled the proponents of Brexit to appeal simultaneously to the notion of an independent, 'buccaneering Britain', freed from the regulatory shackles of Brussels, while also promising to build back the borders needed to reclaim England for the English after two decades of supposedly uncontrolled migration. The bitter irony is that Brexit has delivered less control, not more – the UK no longer has a seat at the table in Brussels, and has foregone its role as the diplomatic hinge between Washington and the EU. British companies who want to trade with Europe now have to follow rules their politicians no longer have a hand in making; British diplomats trying to broker an end to the 'small boats' crisis have no standing inside the EU to cut a deal on migrant returns; and to keep trade flowing the UK elected not to police its own customs and regulatory border with the EU for three years after Brexit. As the world's challenges become ever more global, Brexit has left the UK looking increasingly parochial.

Understandably, Brexit played on the insecurity of communities that felt they were losing their sense of agency in face of global forces: big tech and social media; flat wages and unaffordable houses; low growth and rising job insecurity; immigration and outsourcing. Those issues have roiled all industrialised democracies in different ways, with differing results. But the original sin of Brexit was to promise that leaving the EU would make the UK better able to meet those challenges. It didn't, it won't – and it was never going to. Those who made those rash promises should have known better. Most of them surely did.

It's time to think again about Brexit by taking an approach based on the facts, not fallacy and fantasy. Both Conservatives and Labour continue to set red lines over the UK's future relationship with Europe – no membership of the customs union or EU single market – while airily promising that the disadvantages of leaving the EU will be massaged away over time. More likely, if those red lines do not at least turn pink, the opposite will be the case as the EU finds other places to do business with; other universities to send their students to; other musicians to play in their orchestras; and other nations through which to thread their supply chains and build security and energy alliances. The process of honestly interrogating Brexit trade-offs does not have to be a counsel of despair. It could just as easily be a wake-up call, helping the UK identify structural shortcomings at home, as much as deciding where to set the cursor on the relationship with the EU. But time is of the essence. The UK's diplomatic and trading relationships with Europe have a half-life. Based on the current rate of attrition, many will not survive another seven years of disengagement and decay. The time for a Brexit reboot is now.

Trade: The Basics

EU trading relationships membership levels at a glance – gold, silver and bronze.

Membership of the EU Single Market

- The 'gold' package. Where goods, services, people and capital all circulate freely. This is what the UK enjoyed as an EU member.

- To make that happen, all members of the market sign up to a 'common rulebook' on goods. This means that you can throw a box of sausages into a van in Birmingham and drive it to Berlin, confident that all the other countries are following the same rules and regulations.

- When goods cross the border within the EU there are no customs or other checks to ensure you are conforming to the regulations – because it is presumed these are being enforced by each member internally and at the external borders of the EU.

- To ensure the rules are being enforced equitably and preserve a 'level playing field' for trade, the members of the market also agree to abide by the rulings of a common court – the European Court of Justice – in areas where this is necessary to allow the free movement of goods and services.

- Within the EU the single market is underpinned by the Customs Union. This means that goods entering from outside the single market pay the same tariff – a common external tariff – in order to ensure no one is undercutting each other. But once that tariff is paid, the goods can circulate freely among all the members, regardless of where they were made, so no customs checks are needed.

- Members of the market also agree not to treat each

other's workers differently – Polish or Portuguese citizens have the same rights to live and work around the EU as German or French citizens.

- EU members also make financial contributions to pay for the workings of the EU's collective institutions – the EU Commission, Council and Parliament. Some funds are redistributed directly to poorer regions in order to strengthen the economic foundations of the Union.

- The EU single market is still incomplete in many respects, particularly in services. The EU is looking to further harmonise rules on tax, transport, energy and medicines to further facilitate trade. The 'digital' single market looks to harmonise rules on areas like data, copyright and telecoms.

- You can be in the EU's single market, but not in the EU – which is what Norway, Iceland and Liechtenstein do as members of the European Economic Area (EEA). But they must accept the common rules without having a say in how they are made, and pay financial contributions. Their goods are subject to customs checks at the border since only locally produced goods are duty-free.

Membership of the Customs Unions, But Without a Single Market

- The silver option. Under the EU customs union all the members of the EU customs territory agree to charge the same tariff, with the customs authorities of all EU countries working together as if they were one.

- Once the EU's common external tariff is paid on goods, they can then circulate freely within the Union. Therefore no customs duties are charged when goods cross, say, from France to Germany or from Italy to Spain.

- The EU customs union is made up of EU members, but the EU has a partial customs union with Turkey, which covers industrial goods, but not agricultural products. Turkey aligns with EU rules on goods covered by its customs union with the EU.

- Membership of a customs union with the EU still does not remove all border checks related to the single market. That would also require a full 'regulatory union' and an agreement from the EU to recognise that the UK was qualified to certify goods as compliant with the rules of the EU single market.

A Free Trade Agreement

- The bronze package. The EU–UK Trade and Cooperation Agreement (TCA) is a comprehensive free trade agreement that covers goods and a strictly limited number of services, but falls far short of either EU single market membership or a customs union with the EU.

- Although the deal is a 'zero-tariff, zero-quota' agreement, this does not mean that all UK goods automatically enter the EU tariff-free. To avoid paying tariffs, UK exporters must prove their goods are sufficiently 'locally made' to qualify for that tariff-free access.

- The trade deal lays down complex rules that firms must follow – 'rules of origin' – specifying exactly how to calculate whether a good is sufficiently 'local' to enter tariff-free. This takes time and generates paperwork. Goods without sufficient 'originating content' pay tariffs.

- But tariffs are only one small element of what restricts trade across borders – differing regulations and restrictions on travel and recognising professional qualifications ('non-tariff barriers' to trade) can be a much greater drag on cross-border exchange.

- The TCA is not a regulatory union, so goods arriving at the border also have to show they comply with a wide range of EU rules and regulations, from packaging to organic food standards.

- Crucially, even if the UK follows the EU's regulations and standards, it still must demonstrate that it has done so – that means lots of paperwork and certification. Unilateral alignment with EU rules doesn't remove the need for this paperwork and checks.

- The UK is also no longer part of the EU's common VAT framework, which means exporters need to pay VAT on goods as they arrive in the EU, which often requires employing a 'fiscal representative' to pay the tax on the goods.

- The TCA also provides for very limited access to the EU for financial and business service providers when compared to membership of the EU single market. That means UK professionals – from ski instructors and musicians to engineers and architects – can no longer operate in the EU without visas and permits.

- UK banks also no longer enjoy 'passporting' rights, giving them equal access in the EU markets. Maintaining data flows between the EU and the UK relies on a unilateral decision by the European Commission that UK data protection standards are equivalent to the EU's.

Part I

What Went Wrong With Brexit

I

Fuck Business

One of the most counter-intuitive impacts of Brexit is how the Conservative Party – the self-proclaimed 'party of business' – quickly found itself so deeply at odds with the business establishment. The clash was inevitable since reclaiming sovereignty from Brussels and the European Court of Justice – neatly summarised by Boris Johnson as 'taking back control of our money, our borders and our laws' – by definition meant quitting the EU's single market. To create a free trade area of 27 separate countries, you need to agree on open borders, a common rule-book and a single arbiter of those rules – the European Court of Justice – in case there is a dispute. But once inside the external boundaries of the EU market, then goods, services, capital and labour – the trucks, the service providers, the money and the data that make up the lifeblood of modern trade – can circulate freely. Brexit puts the UK outside that marketplace, acting like a tourniquet, constricting the arterial flow of goods and services across the English Channel and making the UK less attractive to international investors who previously used the UK as a gateway for their operations into Europe. From car makers to chemical factories, clothing importers to machine-makers, the UK, with its English language, strong institutions and open investment climate, had long provided the perfect staging-post for international businesses looking to enter the EU.

For many businesses, Brexit took much of that away and, as a result, put the government unavoidably at loggerheads with those who were responsible for moving and making things. Not surprisingly, business groups like the CBI and the British Chambers of Commerce declined to embrace the idea of building back borders with their nearest and closest market in exchange for the vague promise of a 'buccaneering Britain' and a new deregulatory nirvana. They didn't need a crystal ball to see it wouldn't work; the cost–benefit analysis was so obviously negative. This reluctance frustrated politicians who didn't want those inconvenient truths to complicate their promise that Brexit would 'unchain Britannia'. Sometimes those frustrations boiled over. In 2018, as the UK still groped towards a Withdrawal Agreement with Brussels, Boris Johnson, at the time the foreign secretary, was asked why the needs of business were being ignored by Brexiters. His response was, 'Fuck business!' (Johnson later clarified he only meant 'big business', which is ironic, since his Brexit, as we shall see, did far more to damage small businesses than large ones.)

And indeed 'fuck business' is pretty much what happened. The Conservative Party's obsession with removing the writ of the European Court of Justice from all aspects of the UK's future relationship with the EU put a thick red line through a long list of things that facilitated frictionless trade between the UK and the EU. Logically, the collaborative umbrella that the EU threw over many sectors of the economy required cross-border agencies, like the European Medicines Agency (once based in London), to regulate that trade. Membership of those agencies required countries to pool a measure of their national sovereignty and abide by the judgments of a supranational, pan-European court. For ultras on the Tory Eurosceptic Right this was an intolerable intrusion over the authority of the national Parliament in Westminster. They argued that accepting laws from Brussels was fundamentally undemocratic, even though successive British governments, officials and elected representatives had had an outsized say in the making of those rules via their membership of the Brussels institutions – the European Council, Commission and Parliament.

So, as he built a blueprint for a new trading relationship with the EU in early 2020, David Frost, the UK's chief negotiator, sought total freedom from the judgments of the European Court of Justice at any cost – or more specifically, at the expense of British industry and small businesses. The strange part was that in a previous life, as a former head of the Scotch Whisky Association, which represents one of Britain's most successful exports, Frost had extolled the virtues of the EU single market.

As he explained in an article published just a few weeks before the 23 June 2016 referendum, 'the single set of rules in the single market makes it easier for us to operate across all of Europe', adding that life outside the single market would be 'more complex, burdensome and uncertain'.

He was right about that. And yet fast-forward four years to 2020 and Frost had changed his tune. After entering Downing Street as Johnson's top Europe and Brexit negotiator, the former British diplomat turned political adviser had apparently undergone something of a Damascene conversion. In a speech in Brussels that February, delivered just as EU–UK trade talks were about to get under way, Frost announced that he no longer believed that having a single set of rules covering 500 million wealthy consumers was all that important for facilitating trade. This, despite a mountain of academic studies showing that having divergent regulations, red tape and border bureaucracy – so-called 'non-tariff barriers' – were a major impediment to cross-border commerce. And yet the negotiation was conducted as if only tariffs really mattered and the non-tariff barriers to entering the EU single market could be wished away.

Frost told an audience at ULB Brussels University that 'all these studies exaggerate – in my view – the impact of non-tariff barriers, they exaggerate customs costs, in some cases by orders of magnitude'. This, then, was the basis on which Frost apparently proceeded to negotiate a trade deal that piled non-tariff barriers onto British business. Frost's view was never seriously substantiated but it fitted with the Brexiters' vision of 'global Britain' and a belief that EU membership was the cause of the UK's creeping economic stagnation after 2008. In short, it was the only view that could be squared with the Conservative Party's determination to repatriate undiluted sovereignty from Brussels, but without confronting the economic costs of doing so.

At the same time, in one of his first big Brexit speeches after completing the Withdrawal Agreement, Boris Johnson said the UK wanted only a basic free trade agreement with the EU. He added there was 'no need for a free trade agreement to involve accepting EU rules', claiming that the UK would maintain or even exceed EU standards in many areas but 'without the compulsion of a treaty'. But Johnson's offer of voluntary alignment fundamentally ignored how the EU single market actually worked.

Merely promising to follow EU rules without agreeing to accept the same rulebook and referee (the European Court of Justice) as everyone else was never going to deliver the benefits of frictionless trade. It's as if an England football team went to the European Championships and promised to stick to FA rules, at least most of the time, but wouldn't accept the rulings of the UEFA referees, and then demanded to be treated the same as the other teams. Obviously, that wouldn't work. If England was allowed to compete on those terms, it would lead to other teams joining in the free-for-all, causing the entire system to break down. This was why the European Commission was so adamant, at the outset, that the UK could not 'cherry-pick' the rules of the EU single market. Because while the UK might well be aligned today, the EU was extremely mindful that under Johnson's vision for the deal, it was free to diverge tomorrow. You were either in, or you were out.

So, as it turns out, a 'free' trade agreement is something of a misnomer. Unlike the EU Customs Union, where the same tariff is paid at the external border on all goods, which then move freely inside the territory of the customs union, a free trade agreement is considerably more restrictive. Only goods that can prove they are around 50 per cent 'home-made' can enter the EU without paying a tariff. Proving this level of 'originating content' – the so-called 'rules of origin' – takes a lot of paperwork. Even then, this only removes the need to pay the tariff. It does not remove the need for customs declarations and checks, including physical checks on goods at the border. On top of this traders also need all the paperwork to demonstrate that the goods conform with myriad EU regulations covering everything from food production to packaging requirements.

So if the UK was not prepared – like Norway – to follow the EU rules and accept the jurisdiction of the EU's court and regulators, then British businesses and exporters would be subjected to the full panoply of paperwork and proofs each and every time they approached the EU border. And that's exactly what happened when Frost's bare-bones trade deal came into force in January 2021. His belief that the costs of red tape were 'exaggerated' turned out, unsurprisingly, to be unfounded. 'Brussels red tape' – that had for so long been the object of

British Eurosceptic derision – now tied UK traders in knots. Data from HM Revenue and Customs shows that export declarations by UK businesses more than tripled in the year after the UK left the EU single market and customs union. Businesses were left filling out myriad forms in order to move goods which – before Brexit – had moved as easily between Birmingham and Barcelona as they had between Birmingham and Bristol. Not any longer. The paperwork was so challenging that a vast number of smaller businesses simply gave up trying to trade with Europe. A study by the LSE's Centre for Economic Performance found that the number of relationships connecting UK sellers and EU buyers tumbled by a third after the introduction of the EU–UK trade deal in January 2021.

One of the biggest casualties of the 'back to basics' approach to trade with the EU was the food and drink industry. Checks on animal and plant products are the most cumbersome and long-winded at any border because they are critical to the EU's biosecurity and the protection of animal and human health. The EU takes these checks very seriously. The Brexiters' desire to be free from European food safety rules in order to strike trade deals around the world created yet more barriers to trade. Johnson's negotiating team ruled out any deal with Brussels that required aligning on sanitary and phytosanitary measures (SPS) that regulate plant and animal products. Even though, the day after Brexit, UK rules had not changed one jot, UK exporters still found themselves having to prove this was the case. The result was massive additional bureaucracy that hit food exports across the country, from Scottish salmon producers to Suffolk pig farmers. That put extra cost and customs and port delays on food exports, reducing the shelf-life of perishable products like meat and fish, making them less valuable and attractive to EU customers.

Some companies gave up selling into Europe at all. But many of those that soldiered on, like Hampstead Tea, a boutique maker of organic and biodynamic teas, found that the only way to survive was to shift their distribution networks to the Netherlands, which moved warehousing and distribution for the rest of the world out of the UK. Hampstead Tea was a classic example of a small British business that had flourished and expanded easily into the EU before Brexit suddenly brought the shutters down. The owner, Kiran Tawadey, founded her company 25 years ago after bringing five chests of high-grade Darjeeling tea from her native India and selling the contents in 250g packets to local shops and cafés. By the time of Brexit she was selling 100,000kg of tea a year, with big supermarkets in Italy, France and Germany among her clients. She was braced for bureaucracy after Brexit, but nothing could prepare her for the chaos and complexity of exporting goods to the EU.

Before Brexit, Tawadey imported teas from around the world, cleared customs and plant health controls in the UK port of Felixstowe, and then registered them on the EU's pan-European 'TRACES' database. After that, the products could be distributed freely to all 27 other EU countries. Raw teas could be blended, packed and distributed from facilities in Milton Keynes, dispatched next-day by courier anywhere in the EU. After Brexit, Tawadey wrestled with exporting her products to EU countries for the first three months, but then gave up. Each EU country has a different VAT regime, and even though rules for, say, organic products, are supposed to be standardised across the EU, in practice they can be implemented very differently by different national customs authorities. Because the UK had given up its EU single-market membership, British firms like Hampstead Tea were now treated as outsiders – the UK was a so-called 'third country' that was no longer sheltered by the EU's regulatory umbrella.

Her first consignment to Italy was stuck in customs for eight weeks before it was cleared, angering her clients. After Brexit each consignment of tea to Italy required 'certificates of analysis', and photographs of the product with the outer case; specific stickers containing details of the Italian importer were required for each pallet of goods – or around 12,000 individual units in a single consignment. Some teas that were shipped in bulk packets of over 3kg required customs duties to be paid on them; others, sufficiently transformed by being blended and packed in the UK, could enter the EU tariff-free. This was because, while the UK's trade deal was a 'zero-tariff, zero-quota' deal, only goods that were around 50 per cent 'made in the UK' qualified for zero-tariff access under the so-called 'rules of origin' system.

These problems multiplied in France and Germany to the point where Tawadey had clients raging down the phone. It was, she recalled, 'horrible'. She couldn't honestly blame her clients when they warned her that if she couldn't deliver her products reliably, then the shelf space that was reserved for Hampstead Tea would soon be filled with that of her rivals. The bureaucracy now associated with British products made it much harder to win customers. When Tawadey went to visit a trade show in Germany in the summer of 2021 to drum up fresh business, she found conversations ending abruptly when potential clients realised her trading base was back in the UK. Companies were only interested in partners that were operating inside the EU single market free from the border bureaucracy that gummed up their distribution networks. 'The message was clear,' Tawadey recalled. 'If you don't have an EU entity, don't even bother.'

The situation rapidly became intolerable. Here's a snippet of the kind of mind-numbing correspondence Tawadey engaged in with her customs adviser as she wrestled with the Italian authorities, arguing over whether 'green tea' was a fresh product, and therefore needed to be treated differently to 'black tea':

There does seem to be conflicting information. According to the link that the Italian plant health authority have sent you, commodity code 0902 10 00 refers to 'Tea leaves, fresh, whole, uncut, unfermented, not flavoured'. Having looked at the commodity code from our point of view, 0902 10 00 refers specifically to 'green tea (not fermented) in immediate packings of a content not exceeding 3kg'.

We completely understand why there is confusion surrounding this. As such, we would advise you to reply to the email that you have received from Italy, and ask them to clarify whether or not this means that you require a phytosanitary certificate for all tea being imported to Italy, or just certain types of tea. It may also be worth clarifying if this applies even if the tea is processed, as the description 'Tea leaves, fresh, whole, uncut, unfermented, not flavoured' doesn't clarify this.

So much for non-tariff barriers being 'exaggerated'. In the end Tawadey took the advice of the HM Customs and Excise experts and shifted her business to the Netherlands. It was much easier to go through the entire exporting rigamarole for a bulk consignment and then, having cleared customs and VAT in the Netherlands, distribute freely and in a timely fashion to clients all across the EU single market. Soon after, Tawadey shut down her Milton Keynes warehouse, engaged a third party to blend and pack her teas in the UK and shifted the distribution operation lock, stock and barrel to the Netherlands. Tawadey's UK workforce halved from twelve to six and she paid Dutch corporation tax on her EU business, reducing payments to the UK exchequer. The whole experience made her 'sad and cross'.

But the impact of Brexit is not confined to goods trade: modern commerce is no longer just about shifting boxes of physical products across borders. Increasingly goods and services come highly intertwined, meaning advanced products like engines are supplied with lucrative contracts to provide ongoing support, from servicing to software upgrades. The UK is particularly strong in services – not just financial services, but everything from engineers to architects. Brexit makes life harder for these service-oriented companies because British professionals now need permits to operate in the EU, which puts them at a significant disadvantage when compared to their European competitors. The British Chambers of Commerce estimates that the EU–UK trade deal contains over 1,000 different restrictions on cross-border trade in services, whether EU-wide or at individual country level. For a small business, this creates a bureaucratic minefield. For example, if a Dutch company is looking to get its industrial generator serviced, it can either source an engineer from inside the single market, paperwork-free, or it can spend weeks applying for permits for a British engineer to come and do the job. What makes more sense, hiring 'Roberto' from Italy, or 'Robert' from the UK? It's not hard to see how UK companies will lose out.

Which was exactly the experience of Infinity Engineering Services, a Lincoln-based company that services industrial gas turbine generators. After Brexit the company found itself asking its clients in the Netherlands, Sweden and Italy to obtain work permits for visiting engineers. But the EU companies either refused or couldn't ascertain from their own bureaucracies which permits were required. In the Netherlands, Infinity was told permits could take up to 12 weeks to obtain. That might work for a pre-planned annual service but not for an emergency breakdown. Some EU clients suggested Infinity engineers came and worked illegally using the free '90 days in 180' allowance for UK tourists to the EU, but then asked Infinity to accept legal liability for any infringement if it was discovered in the future. 'The clients would put a disclaimer on the purchase order saying that if we were found in breach, we'd be liable, but I always said, "It's your responsibility,"' said Rob Caruso, customer care manager at Infinity. With so much uncertainty surrounding the rules, three years after Brexit Infinity has almost given up on EU business, which, before Brexit, they targeted as a growth area. Instead they have shifted their attention to Thailand and elsewhere.

These are just two stories from two small British companies, but the experience was replicated all across the UK. And these weren't just teething problems. Some 18 months after the EU–UK trade deal entered into force, a survey of over 2,600 UK exporters by the British Chambers of Commerce revealed that overseas sales growth has been effectively stagnant for more than a year. The chamber's head of trade policy, William Bain, blamed 'the impact of Brexit red tape and compliance costs' for having a 'chilling effect' especially for smaller firms already scarred by the pandemic. That landscape presents huge challenges for the future. Small businesses like Hampstead Tea that expanded easily into Europe before Brexit – as easily as putting products on a website, opening a PayPal account and engaging a courier company – are now separated from that rich market on their doorstep by layers of new bureaucracy. Fewer small businesses will have the opportunity to grow into medium- and larger-sized businesses as a result of Brexit. The pipeline of future UK exporters is at risk. Big business, by contrast, has the in-house bureaucratic muscle to cope with the paperwork, but doing so eats into profits and – for EU companies operating inside the EU single market – makes UK companies more bureaucratic and expensive to deal with.

The majority of analysts say the data suggests the post-Brexit red tape is taking its toll on UK trade. The data for the first two years of Brexit trading remains imperfect, muddied by the one-off global shocks of the Covid-19 pandemic and the war in Ukraine, but erecting barriers to trade with your largest trading partners comes with cost – even if the final size of those costs won't become clear for a decade or more. There is already early evidence of the potential hit from Brexit on UK trade. An analysis of UK trade performance after Brexit by economists at the Resolution Foundation think tank in February 2023, for example, found that, once an unusual spike in gold trading was stripped out of the data, the UK's goods exports at the end of 2022 were nearly 11 per cent below pre-pandemic levels of the same period in 2018.

In March 2023 the independent fiscal watchdog, the Office for Budget Responsibility (OBR), was gloomy about the UK's post-Brexit trade prospects, forecasting 'weak growth in imports and exports over the medium term' that 'partly reflect the continuing impact of Brexit'. One measure of the impact of Brexit is what economists call 'trade openness'. This is the ratio of a country's total exports and imports relative to its GDP. This gives you an indicator of how 'open' that country is to the global trading system. The OBR expects Brexit to reduce the 'overall trade intensity' of the UK economy by 15 per cent in the long term. As the Resolution Foundation and the Centre for Economic Performance at the LSE expressed it in their look at the UK's economic prospects to 2030: 'We should expect the lasting impact of reduced openness to be substantial, and to lead to widespread productivity and real income shocks, much of which has already taken place.'

Taken in the round, the vast majority of economic impact assessments of Brexit are negative. This stands to reason. If removing barriers boosts trade, as we know it does, then re-imposing bureaucratic obstacles with your largest trading partner (which is what the TCA does) will logically reduce that trade. By how much, and to what effect on the wider economy, is less certain. Calculating the 'hit' to long-term UK GDP caused by Brexit over the next 10 to 15 years is an inexact science and results differ depending on the methods used. A 2019 Bank of England assessment forecast a 3.25 per cent negative hit to GDP over 15 years from Brexit; while in March 2023 the OBR said it expected a 4 per cent negative hit to the UK economy, based on a central estimate of a number of different impact studies. Other studies that have taken into account the 'dynamic' impacts of lower productivity caused by reduced trade have estimated the hit will be bigger. The LSE predicted that, depending on the policies the UK government enacted after Brexit, the reduced trade and productivity from Brexit could cause a loss of 6.3 per cent to 9.5 per cent of GDP, or about £4,200 to £6,400 per household.

Forecasts are only forecasts, it is true. One obvious problem is that we never get to live the counterfactual: no one is living in a parallel universe in which Brexit never happened and can report back as to how trade is faring for 'No-Brexit UK'. That's why some economists have built models to try to mimic how the UK might have performed in this alternative reality. They do this by comparing the UK's actual post-Brexit performance with a 'basket' of other economies that have experienced other global factors, like Covid and the Ukraine war energy-shock, but not Brexit. Comparing the UK's actual performance against this hypothetical or 'doppelgänger' UK, John Springford at the Centre for European Reform think tank, estimated Brexit caused a 5.5 per cent negative hit to GDP compared to what might have been if the UK had remained in the EU. Jun Du, Emine Beyza Satoglu and Oleksandr Shepotylo at Aston University used a similar technique to build a 'synthetic' UK economy and found that UK exports to the EU fell by 22.9 per cent in the first 15 months of the TCA, compared to what they otherwise would have been if the UK had remained in the EU.

There is, of course, no perfect crystal ball when it comes to economic forecasts. Brexit is just one variable in a future that will be shaped by known unknowns, like the geopolitical shocks caused by war or the transformative potential of artificial intelligence. But headwinds of Brexit are unique to Britain. All things being equal, the persistent complaints of British businesses about the difficulties of trading with Europe since the TCA came into force is a real-world symptom that leaving the EU is having a negative effect on trade. Still, it should be said that a much smaller number of economists, like Patrick Minford at Cardiff Business School and Graham Gudgin at the Centre For Business Research at Cambridge University, say the consensus around these negative Brexit impacts is flawed. They argue that challenges facing the UK economy are unfairly being blamed on Brexit and that the impact of Brexit, beyond some short-term disruption, has been marginal to non-existent. But despite these dissenting voices, both the Bank of England and the OBR have said that nothing they have seen in the two years since the TCA has come into force has caused them to alter their initial assessments. If anything, the Bank has said, the negative impacts of Brexit are landing faster than expected.

Of course, the vast majority of what was happening was understandably lost on the general public who, from the spring of 2020, were preoccupied with battling Covid-19. When the UK–EU trade deal came into force on 1 January 2021, global trade was so scrambled by the impact of the pandemic that it initially obscured the impact of furring up the pipes of UK trade with the EU. But while the global pandemic took over the news agenda, the economic self-harm being inflicted on the UK economy by Brexit was piling up. It was as if UK plc had been subject to a hostile internal takeover by a charismatic but chaotic new boss who promised he had a magic formula to make UK plc 'great again'. This was based around a highly ambitious global expansion strategy that focused on trade on the other side of the world. But while China is indeed a huge market and growth rates in Asia are enticing, the UK still conducts nearly half its trade with Europe. Eyeing up faraway markets is not the same as accessing them: distance matters when it comes to trade.

It is remarkable to think that the UK plunged headfirst into Brexit without ever producing the national equivalent of a business plan. The entire experiment was predicated on empty but reassuring assertions that had no basis in fact. Business tried to intervene but was waved away. The promise of 'global Britain' was always a chimera. Even the government's most optimistic estimates for the value of post-Brexit trade deals – including a deal with the USA which has not yet materialised – was 0.2 per cent of additional GDP growth in the medium term. That's a tiny sum when set against the costs of hobbling the UK's access to the EU single market. As noted above, the cost of doing so was assessed by the Office for Budget Responsibility to leave the UK economy 4 per cent smaller than it otherwise would have been. Two years after the Brexit trade deal came into force, the OBR said it had seen nothing that made it want to change that assessment.

How on earth were Johnson and Frost allowed to get away with it? Why wasn't there a 'shareholder revolt', demanding that any EU–UK trade deal properly took account of the interests of those who actually did the trading? Partly it was because much of the negotiation revolved around technical nitty-gritty, which made it hard to make the public case for a less destructive course of action. And partly it was the day-to-day distraction of the fallout from the Covid-19 pandemic which consumed many business leaders. Many big business interests and high-profile consumer brands who might have forced a course correction on the Johnson government made a calculated decision to stay out of the political fray. Smaller businesses, which were actually most at risk from a deal that built back trade borders, never had the collective heft to make their voices heard. Those who protested – whether chief executives or Whitehall officials brave enough to question this act of strategic self-harm – were dismissed as 'doomsters', or captives of the 'EU mindset' who could not grasp the glorious opportunities that Brexit presented.

The result was a climate of silence which enabled the Johnson government to negotiate a trade deal which made the UK economy more closed to the outside world, even as they trumpeted the merits of 'global Britain'. It was, Johnson announced excitedly on Christmas Eve 2020 when the deal was signed, a 'Canada-style' deal. That might have sounded impressive to the average viewer who just wanted to get on with wrapping the Christmas presents and stuffing the turkey. But it was nothing of the kind: the value of Canadian goods exports to the EU in 2020 was €20 billion – that's barely *one-tenth* of the value of UK goods exports to the EU that year. By the same token, the coast of Canada is 4,000 miles from the EU; while the UK is separated from Europe by the 27 nautical miles of the English Channel between Dover and Calais. The umbilical link of the Channel Tunnel and the constant stream of roll-on, roll-off ferries makes this one of the most high-intensity trade routes in the world. It takes less than two hours to sail between Dover and Calais, but three weeks to cross the Atlantic.

Still, Johnson breezed that his Canada-style Trade and Cooperation Agreement was a 'fantastic' deal for Britain, but he avoided the obvious question: why on earth would the UK want to trade with the EU on the same terms as Canada? Indeed, that night Johnson told the nation that his 'free'-trade deal would, 'if anything . . . allow our companies and our exporters to do even more business with our European friends'. This was obviously untrue. The fact that Johnson could even say such a thing with a straight face exposed just how fact-free the Brexit debate had become.

2

The Red Tape Fallacy

There is a well-worn story in Whitehall that dates back to the early 1990s when John Major was prime minister, battling the Eurosceptic backbenchers that he dubbed 'the bastards'. As domestic opposition mounted to the ratification of the Maastricht Treaty, opponents seized on an apparently perfect example of Brussels pettifoggery: a 1988 EU directive mandating an upper limit for the number of decibels that could be emitted by a garden lawnmower. From Birmingham to Barcelona, it seemed that the dead hand of the 'Brussels bureaucrat' was inescapable. Even the sovereign right of an Englishman to make as much noise as he pleased when mowing the lawn on a Saturday afternoon was apparently subject to EU control.

As the former *Financial Times* columnist Philip Stephens tells it, furious ministers – including the then foreign secretary Douglas Hurd – demanded an investigation into why British diplomats in Brussels had not intervened to block such an absurd regulation. By their negligence they had handed opponents of European integration yet another stick with which to beat the government. It soon emerged, however, that not only had the UK officials failed to block the lawnmower directive, they had actually conceived it and actively promoted it to other EU member states. The reason? Because German national regulations had set a lower decibel limit, one that excluded noisy British-made lawnmower brands, in what looked suspiciously like an act of protectionism. The much-derided lawnmower directive, therefore, far from stunting the rights of Britain's gardeners, was actually promoting and protecting British exporters through the creation of a level playing field. The genesis of the directive was also a reminder that, contrary to the simplistic notion that such things were imposed by 'unelected bureaucrats' in Brussels, they were created at the behest of member states, if a qualified majority of votes from national governments could be obtained.

But despite the attractive simplicity of a single set of rules applying across national borders to smooth the passage of trade, the idea never took root in the British public imagination. On the contrary. Even as borders and barriers fell away after 1992 as the EU single market deepened, the threat of Brussels regulation was constantly held up as an affront to British sovereignty. This was fuelled by a litany of newspaper stories of the genre in which Boris Johnson excelled as a correspondent for the Brussels bureau of the *Daily Telegraph*. In an alternative universe, those same EU regulations, rather than being demonised for suffocating native British individualism and ingenuity, might have been lauded as the bureaucratic oil that greases the wheels of trade, boosting productivity, creating higher-quality jobs and growing UK export opportunities.

Because this is actually what happened. UK companies from car makers to chemical manufacturers integrated their supply chains during the period of the UK's membership of the EU. British companies were exposed to competition with their European peers, which had a positive impact on productivity. Research by Professor Nicholas Crafts, an economic historian at Warwick University, found that the gain from joining the EU was around 10 per cent of GDP, which exceeded the costs of membership by a ratio of around seven to one. A major reason for this outcome, Crafts found, was a significant increase in competition. This, of course, didn't mean that Brussels' one-size-fits-all regulation was perfect, or that it wasn't costly or sometimes irritating – and that business didn't sometimes campaign against it. But on balance, it produced benefits.

Unfortunately British Euroscepticism never managed to wrap its collective mind around the idea that British business, far from being strangled by Brussels 'red tape', was actually a net beneficiary of the common standards the UK had actively helped to create. These were often to its advantage, as the lawnmower story illustrates. These standards facilitated trade across 28 (now 27) countries to create the richest single trading bloc in the world. And yet the false narrative that Brussels bureaucracy was holding Britain back was so deeply ingrained that it coloured both the EU referendum campaign and the increasingly desperate search for 'Brexit opportunities' that has unfolded since.

The reality about Brussels regulation has always been more prosaic. Fast-forward more than 20 years from the Whitehall row over German lawnmowers to 2010. David Cameron was facing his own Eurosceptic rebellion, so he commissioned a comprehensive audit of where Brussels regulation impinged unnecessarily on the UK to identify targets for reform. The so-called 'EU Balance of Competences Review' took two years to complete and ran to 32 reports on all areas of EU activity, drawing on nearly 2,300 pieces of written evidence. David Frost, then a civil servant in the Foreign Office, even helped to write the chapter on the EU single market. But there's a reason why almost no one outside Whitehall has ever even heard of the results of Cameron's review: it didn't find anything much to support the Eurosceptic theory that the UK was being throttled by EU red tape. Yes, business often argued for a more proportionate, lighter-touch approach (as they do with all regulation), but there was no smoking gun.

And yet, come the 2016 Brexit referendum campaign, the idea that the UK would be more prosperous and productive when freed of Brussels red tape was a key part of the 'sell' to Leave voters. Eurosceptics liked to tell scare stories about Brussels edicts to reduce the wattage of vacuum cleaners, kettles and toasters. But contrary to fears that this would lead to weedy suction and interminable waits for the great British cuppa, these restrictions forced manufacturers to find ingenious energy-saving solutions to produce the same results (an example of how regulation can drive innovation, not suffocate it). And yet on the campaign trail in 2016 Boris Johnson was still trotting out the old stories about 'bendy bananas' and claiming that Brussels regulation was costing British business £600 million a week. Except that it wasn't. That alarming figure was taken from an assessment by the Open Europe think tank, but what Johnson neglected to mention was that the same report estimated EU regulation was actually worth £1.1 billion a week in value-add to UK business. Or a net upside of about £487 million a week in a worst-case scenario.

So on one level, Brexiters can't be blamed for failing to find a transformative post-Brexit deregulatory fillip for the British economy, since those benefits never existed in the way that they supposed. One reason for this was that the UK was already a comparatively low-regulation economy when it was a member of the EU, with less onerous requirements for setting up businesses, hiring staff and regulating industries than much of Europe. In a report issued before the Brexit vote the Organisation for Economic Co-operation and Development (OECD) pointed this out, warning that while it would be possible to pursue further deregulation outside the EU, 'the gains would be limited'.

In truth, some of those who would go on to become leading figures in the post-Brexit political landscape knew this perfectly well. Liz Truss, who as UK agriculture minister campaigned for Remain in 2016 but went on to win her premiership by pandering to the hardest Brexiters in her party, set out the challenges with admirable clarity in a speech to the Food and Drink Federation trade lobby on the eve of the 2016 referendum vote:

> That is why that EU market is so precious; because we share the same regulations, we share the same rules over things like food safety, over animal health and welfare – over bottles – and the whisky industry and I have been doing a bit of a UK tour recently. And the whisky industry will tell you how important it is, that because we share those regulations over bottling and labelling, they can simply export their products to Paris just as easily as they can sell them in a supermarket in Preston.

That, of course, is the same Liz Truss who later campaigned for the premiership with the promise to rip up nearly 4,000 pieces of EU-derived law on the UK statute book by the end of 2023.

Understanding the enduring fallacy about EU red tape is an important element in understanding why Brexit has gone wrong. It was always back-to-front to view the EU's common rulebook as 'regulation' – in fact, replacing 28 individual sets of national rules by a single rule was 'de-regulation'. The dogged pursuit of the belief that 'removing EU red tape' would deliver an economic boost, in the face of all the evidence to the contrary, has led successive Conservative governments to take increasingly demented positions on the issue. This matters because certainty over the regulatory environment is absolutely essential for business confidence and for the investment that drives productivity and prosperity in the UK. For them, the last seven years have been endlessly turbulent, which is reflected in the fact that the amount that businesses have invested in the UK since 2016 has flatlined.

But as it has become increasingly obvious that Johnson and Frost's deal is damaging British trade, not enhancing it, many Brexiters have clung ever more tightly to the hope that regulatory divergence could deliver dividends. It became a way to look past the evident failings of the present and still promise a more prosperous post-Brexit future. It has also tied them in knots.

Soon after Boris Johnson took office in 2019 he appointed former Tory leader and long-time Brexiter Iain Duncan Smith, alongside Theresa Villiers and George Freeman, to lead a 'Taskforce on Innovation, Growth and Regulatory Reform' or (TIGRR) to investigate how the UK could 'reshape its approach to regulation and seize new opportunities from Brexit with its newfound regulatory freedom'. It sounded exciting, but the private sector response was tepid indeed, as business leaders repeated their mantra that what they wanted was not deregulation but smart regulation. As the CBI business lobby group put it in early 2023: 'We don't want a bonfire of regulations for business, or divergence for the sake of it. This is about becoming something altogether smarter – and better – for our competitiveness.' Still, after the TIGRR report was filed, Whitehall departments were then set the task of identifying the first wave of 'Brexit opportunities' which David Frost announced in the autumn of 2021. It was telling that the lead item on the government's list was the reintroduction of the crown stamp on pint glasses in British pubs (which actually hadn't been banned by the EU in the first place). The official government document promised reforms 'allowing publicans and restaurants to voluntarily embrace this important symbol on their glassware'. Nigel Farage, the former UKIP leader, said he was 'delighted' by the proposal, which was perhaps the point. Of course, there was more to the TIGRR document than this. There were some interesting ideas about how the healthcare regulators could work to drive innovation in clinical trials and the wider NHS. But it was telling that the chieftains of Brexit chose to trivialise their own project by leading on an item that, as no doubt intended, got plenty of coverage in the same newspapers that had spent decades berating Brussels for its bendy bananas. This is what the trade policy expert Sam Lowe called 'performative divergence' – it's just for show. Brexiters demand their deregulation project is taken seriously, but have too often been unwilling to be serious about it themselves.

It could all be dismissed as a dark political joke if it wasn't costing the economy so badly. The dogged pursuit of the fallacy that deregulation will make the UK productive again has driven post-Brexit Conservative governments to ever-more entrenched positions. Business chiefs are asked by the Business Department for lists of regulations they want tossed on the Brexiters' bonfire, but instead of a great hooray from the CEOs, ministers get only shaking of heads and words of caution. Nearly three years after Brexit proper, the penny still doesn't seem to have dropped that business overwhelmingly wants certainty, particularly when it comes to existing regulation they've already invested in complying with. Juergen Maier, the former chief executive of the UK division of Siemens, the German industrial conglomerate, put it very clearly to a BBC *Question Time* audience in March 2023: 'In the practical sense I don't know of a business that is a trading and an exporting business – and I've worked for a very large one – that believes that diverging from regulation of the European Union makes sense.'

And yet, as the UK prepared to leave the EU single market at the end of 2020 Boris Johnson said: 'We have taken back control of laws and our destiny. We have taken back control of every jot and tittle of our regulation. In a way that is complete and unfettered.' That sounds great, but the reality is the complete opposite. It is a bitter irony that the act of leaving the EU actually left the UK more impacted by EU rules and regulation, not less. And not just because of all that paperwork at the border. When the UK was a member of the EU it had a seat at the table and the chance to push for lighter-touch rules. But once outside, that was gone. Any British business wanting to sell goods into the EU market of 450 million consumers would have to follow EU rules, whether they liked it or not. Having 'nimbler' British rules was of no benefit if you had to go to the expense of complying with EU ones anyway. In fact, managing two regulatory regimes was far more expensive and cumbersome than having a common rulebook.

Which is why, in practice, the UK has actually diverged very little from EU rules since Brexit. In many areas, the UK has become a de facto taker of EU rules. Because while building your own bespoke regulatory regime on, say, gene editing might confer a notional advantage for UK business, the reality is that any upside must be offset against the costs of divergence. It takes time and money to build a new regime – you need to draw up the rules and then staff expensive regulators to carry them out. This is why British attempts to introduce new home-grown regulatory regimes for chemicals, industrial products and medical devices have all been repeatedly delayed. Before Brexit, the burden of managing regulation was shared by 28 countries through agencies like the European Medicines Agency (EMA) or European Chemicals Agency (ECHA) that pooled resources and expertise. Those agencies have international respect and their imprimatur carries huge weight for a business seeking to get a product to market in other jurisdictions.

Now the UK is on its own, its individual regulators will need to re-establish their reputations internationally. The UK also needs, if it is going to have new regulations, sufficient domestic capacity to test whether products conform to those standards – so-called 'conformity assessment' bodies. The Commons Public Accounts Committee which monitors government spending has found that shortages of professionals from vets to toxicologists and lawyers meant that regulators have struggled to stand up new regimes. The Committee found that the Health and Safety Executive had required staff at the agency's Chemicals Regulation Division to spend a quarter of their time in training as they tried to build a bespoke UK chemicals regulation regime that the industry has repeatedly said is costly and unwanted. As PAC chair Dame Meg Hillier put it, 'the result is exposure of UK consumers and businesses to greater risks and costs'.

So for many industries – cars, chemicals, pharmaceuticals, aerospace and precision manufacturing that relied on EU supply chains and sold into EU markets (and were therefore required to conform to EU rules anyway) – there is precious little upside to separate, lighter-touch UK regulation. Rules that cover a market of just 55 million people make no sense when companies have to conform to EU rules in order to serve a lucrative market of 450 million people. It was not, as we shall see, that the UK couldn't find some incremental benefits from improved domestic regulation, but given that almost half the UK's trade is with the EU, those upsides will not outweigh the costs of leaving the EU single market. As one despairing UK industry CEO said to me: 'I just don't understand how they can't understand this?'

But apparently they don't. Take cars. The UK car industry exports 80 per cent of its output, half of which goes to the EU, and therefore relies on following global regulatory standards in order to access markets and keep down costs. After Brexit, the UK government remains committed to creating its own regulatory regime – so-called type approvals – for vehicles entering the UK market, but was repeatedly forced to delay the introduction of the compulsory UK scheme, under pressure from industry. At the same time, the EU has introduced its European General Safety Regulation which includes requirements for new safety technologies, like speed limiters, that send Brexiters into fits of apoplexy about EU nanny statism. Brexiter ministers have suggested British car makers will be free not to adopt such technologies, but the assumption in industry is that the government will quietly adopt these standards. That's because it's not economic to make UK cars to different standards than EU ones – but also, presumably, because it's not a good look politically to argue that British cars should be less safe than European ones. The point is that these deregulatory red herrings distract from where UK industry might actually steal a narrow advantage, for example by having a lighter-touch regulatory regime around the testing of autonomous (self-driving) vehicles and sharing the data generated by them.

Not that any of this has deterred the Brexiters. In fact, despite all the demands from business for continuity they have dogmatically pursued their red tape fantasy. Playing to the gallery, Jacob Rees-Mogg, the business minister under Boris Johnson, took to the pages of *The Sun* newspaper in February 2022 to say: 'I want *Sun* readers to write to me and tell me of ANY petty old EU regulation that should be abolished.' Then the following June he announced that Whitehall had set up a 'dashboard' so that all EU law on the UK statute book could be scrutinised by the public. Anyone who has tried to wade through such regulations would know Rees-Mogg's offer to *Sun* readers was yet another example of 'performative divergence'. Unless you're a professional, EU regulations are next to unreadable.

And yet Rees-Mogg claimed to MPs that reforming such laws 'will create a crucial boost to productivity and help us bring the benefits of growth to the whole country'. However, the government has never produced a substantive economic rationale for this claim. That is perhaps because, as Thomas Sampson, an associate professor of economics at the London School of Economics who has modelled the effects of Brexit on UK trade, observed at the time, there is no economic basis for the assertion that cutting EU regulation would deliver a 'crucial boost' to productivity. As he put it at the time: 'Since 2016 the government has failed to identify any changes to EU regulations that would make a substantial difference to productivity growth. There is no reason to believe that the latest initiative will change that fundamental fact.'

But still Brexiters continued to drive the deregulation bandwagon. In September 2022 Liz Truss's government introduced the 'Retained EU Law Bill', a piece of legislation that promised to 'review or revoke' nearly 4,000 pieces of EU-derived law by the end of 2023. Critics rightly called the plans a Brexiter 'vanity project' and a 'make-work scheme' for Whitehall officials and government departments. But it's worse than that: to business chiefs deciding whether to spend money in the UK, a threat to rip up so many of the rules and regulations that underpin commercial life becomes a massive deterrent to investment. This is not to say that the UK shouldn't consider changing some EU-derived laws after Brexit. Now the UK is outside the regulatory orbit of Brussels, the sovereign British Parliament is free to change any EU-derived law it likes, subject to its other international commitments. But as an amazingly broad spectrum of interests warned after the legislation was tabled, a pell-mell rush to expunge the last trace of EU law from the UK statute book would lead to legal uncertainty and massive expense.

Under the legislation proposed by Rees-Mogg, any law that hadn't been either actively saved or junked by the end of 2023 would simply drop off the statute book, leaving a legal vacuum in its place. EU-derived legislation that was sucked onto the UK statute book at the point of Brexit in order to preserve legal continuity covers all areas of life, from workers' rights to cybersecurity, conservation laws to construction regulations. Instead of a methodical, case-by-case approach, the Bill as originally conceived risked a frenetic slash-and-burn approach that has no support among business groups, charities, conservationists, workers' unions or the legal profession. The president of the Law Society warned the impact could be 'devastating'. The chair of the Bar Council said the Bill, as originally conceived, would 'damage the UK's reputation for regulatory stability' and undermine the competence 'on which growth-promoting investment depends'. The Retained EU Law Bill became a dismal advert for Brexit Britain and it was no surprise when Rishi Sunak's government announced a climbdown in May 2023 and ditched Rees-Mogg's original end-of-year deadline.

If the UK government wants to restore the country's battered credibility with investors, the fantasy of an instant, post-Brexit 'EU red tape dividend' needs knocking firmly on the head. No doubt the UK could be better regulated. No doubt outside the EU there are opportunities for a single country to regulate more nimbly than a bloc of 27. But an approach that demands divergence from EU rules and regulation for its own sake, ignoring the reality that the UK conducts a vast amount of trade with the global regulatory behemoth on its doorstep, is destined to fail.

3

Life in the Political Upside Down

The delivery of Brexit went wrong from the very start. After David Cameron quit as prime minister, Theresa May was installed unopposed by Tory MPs as a compromise candidate after Boris Johnson's candidacy faltered at the eleventh hour. There was no election, no vote and no public discussion about what Brexit might mean or how it might be implemented. May was a Remainer, but as home secretary she had been responsible for creating the Home Office's infamous 'hostile environment' towards immigration – legal and illegal. She had driven a hard bargain with Brussels over parts of the EU's Justice and Home Affairs legislation that were judged too intrusive for Britain, taking advantage of the UK's right to 'opt out' of certain EU rules. As such, May was no Europhile, but equally she had demonstrated a willingness to be pragmatic, for example arguing in favour of the UK rejoining the European arrest warrant in 2014 despite criticism from Eurosceptic backbenchers that the scheme impinged too greatly on UK sovereignty. May judged such measures were worth it, on balance, because they kept Britons safer and allowed the easy extradition of European criminals back to Europe. In short, she was a hardline pragmatist.

Alas, any hopes that May would steer a deeply divided Britain back into the middle ground after the Brexit referendum were dashed by a series of political missteps and a disastrous election result in June 2017 in which she lost her majority, and with it her political agency. May, a politician of integrity but limited communication skills, ultimately turned out to be a deeply flawed prime minister who put the UK on the path to the ultra-hard Brexit that was finally delivered by Boris Johnson in December 2019. Right from the start, the Tory Party was in a state of denial about how difficult it would be to implement the vote after more than 40 years of EU membership. That much became painfully clear after May's first big speech on the subject at the Tory Party conference of October 2016.

It took May a good minute to calm the rapturous Tory Party faithful who had gathered in Birmingham buzzing with excitement about the possibilities that Brexit might hold. Under the slogan 'A country that works for everyone', May set out her stall. She promised that the UK would be a 'fully independent, sovereign country', that would have no truck with 'supranational institutions that can override national parliaments and courts' but at the same time would have 'free trade, in goods and services' for 'global Britain'. As we have seen, that is not how the EU single market works. The speech was a mass of incoherence and inconsistencies that immediately set alarm bells ringing in Brussels and with senior UK officials, like the UK's then permanent representative to the EU, Ivan Rogers. In a few clumsy sentences May had slammed the door on a world of different possibilities for the UK's future relationship with Europe and articulated in the most gauche terms the cake-and-eat-it philosophy that would bedevil the next three years of painful negotiations. Rogers, who resigned from his post the following January after his private warnings to ministers about the difficulties that lay ahead were leaked to the BBC, later called it 'the single daftest speech given by any British PM since the war'.

May's speech is now long forgotten, but it is worth recalling if only because it marked the start of a descent into a world of fallacy and wishful thinking that would culminate with the catastrophic 49-day premiership of Liz Truss in the early autumn of 2022. The process of negotiating the UK's exit from the EU brought immense pressure to bear on the UK civil service and judiciary as the Conservative Party tried to reconcile its grand vision for Brexit with reality. Liam Fox's breezy prediction, when he was international trade secretary in 2017, that negotiating a free trade deal with Brussels 'should be one of the easiest in human history' foundered on the failure of British politicians to make the conceptual leap from the UK being a member of the EU – with a seat at the table and the leverage to make demands of Brussels – to being what European negotiators called *'le demandeur'* in a negotiation with a much bigger and more patient adversary. May herself failed mentally to adjust to the UK's new position outside the EU, implying in her speech that the UK would be able to opt in and out of elements of the EU single market, cherry-picking its new relationship with the EU, as had been the case with those Justice and Home Affairs decisions when she was home secretary. And yet Brexit fundamentally changed that world.

When May triggered Article 50 in March 2017, firing the starting gun on the UK's de-accession from the EU, she set a clock ticking that ultimately drove pro-Brexit politics into increasingly extreme positions. Time and again, as May tried to reconcile her promise of frictionless trade with Eurosceptic demands for a clean break with Brussels, she landed on solutions that squared political circles in Westminster but took little account of the trade-offs that leaving the EU entailed, or indeed what was negotiable in Brussels. The results of failing to grasp the European perspective were sometimes embarrassing. David Davis, the then Brexit secretary, promised the 'row of the summer' over the time tabling of the withdrawal talks, a fight that ended with British capitulation inside a week. Boris Johnson then said the EU negotiator Michel Barnier could 'go whistle' for the so-called Brexit bill needed to settle the UK's financial liabilities, but the insouciant Frenchman said he couldn't hear any whistling, just 'the sound of the clock, ticking'. As his senior aide Stefaan de Rynck observed in his account of the negotiations, *Inside the Deal*: 'The UK government played a game of chicken, by itself.'

Entire books have been written about the tumultuous period of the negotiations which would ultimately lead to May's downfall and the installation of Boris Johnson as prime minister in the summer of 2019. The fact that the UK had four Brexit prime ministers in six years tells its own story. Mistakes were made by all sides, including Remainers who failed to accept the outcome of the referendum, but the thread that binds all those administrations is the corrosion of the kind of pragmatic, fact-based policy-making for which the British state had long been justly admired around the world. Instead, British politics has been consumed by magical thinking and dogma which has damaged the UK's reputation not just in Europe but also globally. In 2006, as he became Conservative Party leader, David Cameron had said: 'For years, this country wanted – desperately needed – a sensible centre-right party to sort things out in a sensible way. Well, that's what we are today.' Negotiating Brexit has turned the 'sensible' party into anything but. The so-called party of 'law and order' has become the party that is openly prepared to break international law; the self-professed 'party of business' has become a party that throughout the negotiations, refused to listen to what business had to say. The party of conservatism has become a party of revolution.

Ultimately, May did make a belated accommodation with Brexit reality, constructing a Withdrawal Agreement 'divorce deal' that sought to protect British business by remaining inside a de facto customs union with the EU and avoiding a return to a hard border in Northern Ireland. But by then it was too late. Boris Johnson came to power promising to 'Get Brexit Done', which he duly did by ignoring the trade-offs involved. Rather than grapple with the real-world effects of erecting barriers to the market that takes half UK trade, Johnson and his negotiator David Frost, as we have seen, just wished them away. And when the bare-bones deal was done, Johnson simply denied the downsides. That message worked wonders on a weary British electorate at the general election of December 2019, but as time has passed since Johnson's trade deal came into force in January 2021 public opinion has unsurprisingly curdled as its limitations have become clear.

The costs of that journey have not been confined to the economic fallout from signing a wholly inadequate trade deal with Europe. The job of 'getting Brexit done' has at times stretched the bonds of sound and legal government to breaking point. When in late 2016 High Court judges ruled that MPs should have a say in triggering the Article 50 mechanism, the *Daily Mail* infamously put them on the front page under the headline 'Enemies of the People'. The *Daily Telegraph* framed the debate as 'Judges vs the People'. As several legal commentators noted, there was an irony that Brexiters who campaigned so hard to repatriate judicial sovereignty to the UK should be quite so outraged when British judges had ruled on British legal matters.

Nearly three years later, in summer 2019, Boris Johnson decided to 'prorogue' (shut down) Parliament in order that – as his opponents saw it – his Brexit plans could avoid legitimate scrutiny. Again, the irony that Johnson was apparently seeking to bypass the same Parliament that Brexiters had yearned for so long to make sovereign again was not lost on his opponents. His decision divided judicial opinion, but was ultimately ruled illegal by a unanimous decision from the UK Supreme Court handed down live on television by Baroness Hale of Richmond. As she said: 'The decision to advise Her Majesty to prorogue Parliament was unlawful because it had the effect of frustrating or preventing the ability of Parliament to carry out its constitutional functions without reasonable justification.' The large spider brooch she wore that day was taken up as a symbol of resistance to Brexit by some Remainers, which itself spoke to how Brexit had politicised the perception of the role of the judiciary. Rather than being seen to impartially exercise their responsibilities with regards to the law, judges were now painted by the pro-Brexit media as the villains of the piece. In the past, Brexiters had attacked the European judicial system for impinging on British law (which they did, since EU membership logically required the acceptance of the supremacy of EU law in areas where the UK had agreed to follow EU rules), but after Brexit, they turned their fire on British judges too.

In the end, Johnson grudgingly accepted the UK Supreme Court's verdict and put Parliament back to work, but he never apologised and made no effort to disguise the fact that the Supreme Court decision had rankled. Even three years later, in July 2022, in the dying days of his premiership Johnson defended his record in office by telling the Commons, 'With iron determination we saw off Brenda Hale and we got Brexit done.' Hale had actually retired in 2020, having reached the mandatory age for retirement, but the message of Johnson's parting swipe was clear. The judges had tried to thwart the people and Johnson, backed by his popular mandate won at the 2019 election, styled himself as the man who overcame them. Such blatant undermining of the judiciary by a prime minister is not without constitutional costs.

Even more problematic was Johnson's decision in the autumn of 2020 to table legislation that actually threatened to break the law. The Internal Market Bill threatened to rip up the UK's commitments to key elements of the deal on post-Brexit trading arrangements for Northern Ireland that had been agreed in the EU–UK Withdrawal Agreement and enshrined in UK law. But as the legislation said, 'notwithstanding' those earlier treaty commitments, Johnson now threatened to hand ministers powers to ignore them. His minister Brandon Lewis came to the despatch box to admit this was a 'limited and specific' breach of international law. The brazenness of the move was widely condemned, including by senior Conservatives like the party's former leader Michael Howard. He asked whether the Johnson government understood the damage done by sending a minister to the despatch box to admit the UK planned to legislate to break the law – 'words that I never thought I would hear uttered by a British minister, far less a Conservative minister', said Howard, who is himself a KC. He then asked the obvious question: 'How can we reproach Russia or China or Iran when their conduct falls below internationally accepted standards when we are showing such scant regard for our treaty obligations?'

As well as further poisoning the relationship between London and Brussels, this was indeed an unhappy look for 'global Britain': a country looking to establish its reputation as an independent actor outside the EU. The rupture with basic international good practice caused the UK government's top lawyer at the time, Jonathan Jones, KC, to resign as head of the government's Legal Department, a role he had held for six years. Reflecting later for UK in a Changing Europe's Brexit witness archive, Jones summed up why the episode matters: 'It was a very bad moment for this government's, or any government's, relationship with the rule of law, not to mention the hit to our international reputation that goes with it. [It says] we are a country that's prepared to renege on agreements entered into only very recently.' On one level this moment passed – a subsequent negotiation over the Northern Ireland deal avoided the need for the law-breaking clauses of the Internal Market Bill to be enacted – but the scarring is permanent. When future governments seek to renegotiate the relationship with Europe, diplomats are clear that the bad taste left by the Johnson years will linger. As one senior EU official who lived through the negotiation puts it: 'Even if the next government is solid and sensible and committed to good relations, any future agreements will have to be made on the basis that a future British government might be less solid, less sensible. Good government can no longer be taken for granted. That's the sad legacy of the Trump–Johnson era.'

It is not surprising that when politicians exhibit such a cavalier approach to the rule of law that it should bring them into conflict, both with their legal advisers but also the technocratic civil service. From the outset of the Johnson premiership, the civil service were explicitly made a political target; the 'blob' was the derisive catch-all term used by Tory ministers and Brexit campaigners to describe the civil service and the wider liberal establishment that they accused of seeking to thwart the implementation of the vote to leave. Leading ministers like Liz Truss and Jacob Rees-Mogg were happy to paint the 'blob' as not only lazy, useless slackers, but also a devious and obstructive, pro-Remain cabal determined to frustrate Brexit. The Vote Leave campaign chief Dominic Cummings, attacking Theresa May's government in 2018, said their only strategy is 'to "trust officials to be honest", which is like trusting Bernie Madoff with your finances'. These kind of attacks fall outside the long tradition of politicians chafing at bureaucrats that has provided a rich vein of satire, from the Circumlocution Office of Dickens's *Little Dorrit* to the supercilious Sir Humphrey in the 1980s television sitcom classic *Yes, Minister*. It was sinister, divisive and actively designed to transfer the failure of government onto the backs of officials who had no formal right of reply.

When Ivan Rogers quit in 2017, his valedictory email to his staff was prescient about the practical challenges that delivering Brexit would present to civil servants who faced demands from ministers that, from a practical point of view, were often wrongheaded and destructive.

> I hope you will continue to challenge ill-founded arguments and muddled thinking and that you will never be afraid to speak the truth to those in power. I hope that you will support each other in those difficult moments where you have to deliver messages that are disagreeable to those who need to hear them. I hope that you will continue to be interested in the views of others, even where you disagree with them, and in understanding why others act and think in the way that they do. I hope that you will always

provide the best advice and counsel you can to the politicians that our people have elected, and be proud of the
essential role we play in the service of a great democracy.

This was a brave aspiration, but the Brexit fever of the last
seven years has helped to create what Rogers would later call
a 'fundamental lack of trust' between ministers and the upper
echelons of the civil service in successive post-Brexit governments. In Rogers' view this is qualitatively different than in the
Thatcher era where a reforming government often clashed with
the orthodoxies of the day but nonetheless respected the capacity
of civil servants to get the job done. It might be tempting to
dismiss concerns about threats to break the law (which, after
all, were never enacted) and clashes between ministers and civil
servants as nothing more than the internal witterings of
Whitehall, and certainly not something with real-world consequences that would play on the doorsteps at election time. But
the 'move fast and break things' approach to policy-making
since Brexit has rattled investors and damaged the UK's reputation as a reliable place to do business. It began with the
self-styled maverick leadership of Dominic Cummings, who
entered Number 10 as Johnson's chief adviser in July 2019; six
months later he advertised for 'weirdos and misfits' and threatened to 'bin' new recruits 'within weeks' if they didn't fit in.
It was the kind of language that was meant to convey reforming
zeal, but was just unbecoming of a serious organisation. If the
recruitment director of a FTSE 100-listed company had advertised in such terms they'd have rightly been sacked. The fact
that the de facto chief of staff to the 'CEO of UK plc' felt able
to speak in those terms tells its own story.

This confrontational approach to policy-making continued,
both under Boris Johnson and then Liz Truss, after Cummings
was forced out. And it led to real-world consequences. If there
was any upside to the disaster that was the Truss premiership,
it was that it put a price on bad government. The Resolution
Foundation calculated that the government's missteps with the
financial markets were responsible for about £30 billion of
the £60 billion fiscal 'black hole' in the government's
day-to-day finances at the time of her departure. That particular
piece of chaos started with the sacking of Tom Scholar in

September 2022, the most senior civil servant in the Treasury, who had deep contacts in the City. Scholar was deliberately fired immediately after Truss took office, not quietly eased out in favour of an alternative as is customary when ministers want a change of the civil service guard.

Scholar's sacking was intended to send a signal that Truss wanted to challenge 'Treasury orthodoxy', but it turned Scholar into a political pawn by using him as a cipher for that orthodoxy. Truss was actively fuelling the corrosive narrative of Whitehall technocrats versus Brexiter economic revolutionaries remaking Britain outside the EU. Truss and her chancellor, Kwasi Kwarteng – part of a group of free-marketeer Tories whose 2012 manifesto *Britannia Unchained* called for radical deregulation and tax-cutting in a dash for growth – took that thinking to a destructive extreme, leaving lasting scars on the UK's international reputation. As the former deputy prime minister Lord Heseltine observed, the Truss implosion ultimately demonstrated 'the vacuity' of the whole process. Liz Truss, he said, 'was the last gasp of a dying body'.

Except, not quite. Truss's departure from Downing Street in late October 2022 and the arrival of her successor Rishi Sunak did not spell the end of the welter of Brexit-inspired law-making that has damaged the UK's reputation abroad. Trying to reconcile the promises made at the 2016 referendum with the reality of what has followed has driven politicians deeper and deeper into the world of the political upside down, where they say one thing, but the precise opposite is true. We saw this with Boris Johnson's claim that his Brexit trade deal with our largest trade partner would allow the UK to do 'even more business with our European friends'. It obviously won't. But when reality becomes ever more divorced from the promise of what Brexit would deliver, the only answer is to double down, deriding critics who point out inconvenient facts as 'Remoaners' or Brexit 'saboteurs'.

Take one of Rishi Sunak's pet policies – freeports. This is another example of a Brexit policy that has been a triumph of posturing over substance. In November 2016 Sunak wrote a paper for the Centre for Policy Studies think tank called *The Free Ports Opportunity*, declaring the free trade zones could 'play an important role in signalling Britain's openness to the world, as well as reconnecting the nation with its proud maritime history'. Sunak claimed freeports could create 86,000 jobs in the UK, but when the Institute for Fiscal Studies looked at how Sunak had arrived at this number, in a report in 2023, they found the future prime minister had simply taken the number of jobs in US freeports and adjusted them, pro-rata, for the UK workforce. As the IFS observed, the Sunak paper suffered 'from significant methodological flaws'. Still, Boris Johnson made freeports a centrepiece of his 2019 election campaign claiming they would provide a 'massive boost' to the UK economy after the UK had left the EU. In their roles in the Johnson administration as chief secretary to the Treasury and international trade secretary respectively, Sunak and Liz Truss launched a nationwide competition for freeports, saying that they 'capture the essence of this Government's ambition'. To get everyone in the mood, the government's consultation document started with a misty-eyed preamble about the 'Ancient World' where 'Greek and Roman ships – piled high with traders' wines and olive oils – found safe harbour in the Free Port of Delos, a small Greek island in the waters of the Aegean'.

Meanwhile, back in the real world, it was clear that in economic terms freeports were destined to be empty vessels. Traditionally, freeports work by allowing businesses to import components and ingredients duty-free, use them to manufacture goods, and then pay the tariff on finished products when they are exported either into the domestic economy or abroad. Exploiting the difference, or 'wedge', between the higher tariffs on inputs and lower tariffs on finished products is known as 'tariff inversion'. Sunak's Treasury consultation document cited 'duty inversion' as a key benefit of freeports, but research by the UK Trade Policy Observatory found that under the UK Global Tariff introduced after Brexit 'only around 1 per cent' of UK imports by value could benefit from the inversion opportunity. There was no duty inversion opportunity.

Not surprisingly, when the independent fiscal watchdog, the Office for Budget Responsibility, came to assess the potential of freeports to increase GDP, it found it to be close to non-existent. Based on previous freeport schemes around the world, the OBR said the likely effect of freeports would be to shift existing commercial activity away from one part of the UK to another. Past experience suggested that the Treasury tax breaks on offer to companies setting up inside the new freeport zones is likely to end up subsidising significant amounts of economic activity that would have taken place anyway. Any positive impact on GDP was likely to be so small, the OBR concluded, that 'such effects would probably be difficult to discern even in retrospect'. The IFS also concluded that, at a national level, 'the impacts will almost certainly be very small', even if areas hosting freeports saw a localised increase in activity. But hardly the 'massive boost' Johnson promised.

It's not just on the economy that striving to fulfil over-ambitious Brexit promises has led to weak and misleading policy. On the 2016 campaign trail Brexiters promised to 'take back control' of the UK's borders, but since leaving the EU there has been an upsurge in so-called 'small boat' migration across the Channel as people-smuggling gangs went into overdrive. Leaving the EU was never going to solve an issue which pre-dated joining it. Indeed, to the extent that Brexit led to a significant worsening of relations with France – partially patched up by Rishi Sunak – it has actually made it harder to tackle the problem. When it came to borders, Brexit had primarily been about ending the rights of EU citizens to move freely to live and work in the UK. But since the campaign took place shortly after the 2015 migration crisis, that issue became conflated with responding to refugee crises, asylum seekers and illegal economic migration. Boris Johnson and Michael Gove said during the campaign that Brexit was 'the only way to avoid having common borders with Turkey', which they well knew was a very distant prospect given that Turkey's accession talks with the EU opened in 2005 and had gone nowhere by 2016. And in any case, as an EU member the UK held a veto over Turkish accession.

Considerably less subtly, Nigel Farage had used a photograph of refugees crossing Europe for his infamous 'Breaking Point' poster, creating a fearful impression that the official Leave campaign never officially endorsed but did nothing to dispel. So when the small boat crossings surged, the post-Brexit governments have found themselves under political pressure from core voters to stop them. The pressure was all the greater because they had allowed Brexit voters to believe that leaving the EU would make it easier to control illegal migration across the Channel. This, even though leaving the EU also meant leaving the EU's Dublin Agreement that enabled member states to return migrants to their first safe point of entry in the bloc.

To create a counter-narrative and give the impression of action, in April 2022 the Johnson government came up with a plan to deport new arrivals to Rwanda where their asylum claims would be processed. This idea, which won approval among Conservative voters, went down badly in European capitals. Then, just as the first flights were preparing to leave that June, they were blocked by a ruling of the European Court of Human Rights in Strasbourg – an institution that Conservative Eurosceptics have long disliked for impinging on British judicial sovereignty. The ECHR isn't actually part of the EU, but is underpinned by the 'Convention for the Protection of Human Rights and Fundamental Freedoms' which is signed by 46 member states of the Council of Europe, a much broader group of European nations, which includes the UK.

The UK asylum system is visibly struggling to cope with the small boats crisis, partly because of a shortage of staff needed to process claims swiftly. But the response of the Sunak government was to revive the idea of a new 'British Bill of Rights', which it sold to the media as a solution to the meddling ECHR. Or as *The Sun* put it, 'plans for Bill of Rights to trump Euro laws and crack down on illegal immigration'. The paper went on to claim that the bill 'will finally allow the government's flagship plan to deport Channel migrants to Rwanda to take off after meddling Euro judges blocked it'. Except that in reality – as even some conservative commentators like Henry Hill at the Conservative Home website acknowledged – the bill wouldn't do anything of the sort. It's not that the UK's ECHR membership doesn't throw up legal conflicts for British courts, but as Hill observed, the legislation did not address those issues, but opted instead for 'shouty, sloppy, big-bang reforms made with an eye on the headlines'. Lord Pannick, KC, the eminent human rights lawyer, observed, 'If this Bill were being sold in the shops the Lord Chancellor, in my view, would be at risk of prosecution for false or deceptive advertising.' Any government producing legislation that attracts such derision from the most eminent legal minds in the country should be asking questions of itself. As Baroness Kennedy, KC, noted, passing such a bill would put the UK beyond the pale in the eyes of the rest of Europe where the rights of some 700 million people are protected by the ECHR. 'It is putting us in the company of people such as Orbán, Hungary's premier. We will become an outrider on human rights when we do this,' she said.

But despite all the briefings and hullabaloo, the reality is that for as long as the UK remains a member of the Council of Europe and a signatory to the ECHR, then domestic legislation cannot release the British government from its international treaty obligations. And the reality, as the government admitted when pressed, is that the UK is not going to leave the ECHR because doing so would imperil the UK's international reputation and unravel both the security chapters of the EU–UK Trade and Cooperation Agreement and the Good Friday Agreement, both of which are predicated on continued ECHR membership. In short, as one Whitehall insider memorably put it in the summer of 2022, the Bill promised to be 'red meat' to *Sun* readers, but was actually nothing more than a 'vegan steak'. The Illegal Migration Bill, a proposed change in law that brought the Rwanda deportation policy back into play, which the government admits may breach ECHR commitments, is cut from similar cloth, with much the same political intent. Which is presumably why the Conservative Party sent an email to party activists auto-signed by the home secretary Suella Braverman crowing that: 'We tried to stop the small boat crossings without changing our laws. But an activist blob of left-wing lawyers, civil servants and the Labour Party blocked us.'

The attempt to 'review or revoke' all of the 4,000 pieces of EU-inherited legislation by the end of 2023 via the deceptively drearily titled Retained EU Law Bill was another example of how Brexit has demented British government. It wasn't just lawyers, business groups, conservationists, charities, trade unions and devolved administrations in Cardiff and Edinburgh which all warned the bill was, as the chair of the British Safety Council put it, 'ill-conceived' and could leave a 'legal black hole' in the statute book. The government's own Regulatory and Policy Committee (RPC), which independently assesses whether the government has done its homework on the impacts of legislation, described the Business Department's impact assessment as 'not fit for purpose'. In an extraordinary indictment of the poverty of decision-making behind the legislation, the Committee concluded: 'The Department has not sufficiently considered, or sought to quantify, the full impacts of the Bill. In addition, the [impact assessment] does not include a consideration of the impact on small and micro businesses (SMBs) consistent with Better Regulation.' Even on the Brexiters' own terms, seeking to deliver better regulation outside the EU single market, the bonfire Bill was deemed a failure.

Perhaps this is just the nature of contemporary populist politics, but there should be no illusion: this kind of legislation tarnishes the UK's international reputation. Threats to break international law and rip up rules on which 40 years of common understandings are built unsettles European capitals and feeds into a narrative in parts of the European media that the UK is at risk of becoming a state that cannot be trusted. Some of that commentary is hysterical and overblown, but during the Brexit years it has become increasingly common to hear US and European diplomats ask the question, as much in sorrow as in anger: 'What on earth is going on with the UK?'

Brexit may have exposed shortcomings in Whitehall, but politicians in successive post-Brexit governments must shoulder much of the blame for the dysfunction, tabling legislation that was often performative in nature and stretched the boundaries of what was legal. Civil servants find themselves in an invidious position when they are pushing through legislation, like the Retained EU Law Bill, that is 'red-rated' by the government's own watchdog as 'not fit for purpose'. But as Jill Rutter, the civil service expert at the Institute for Government, has noted, the political chaos of the Brexit years has allowed the civil service 'to hide behind ministers and not take responsibility for its failures'. The perpetual political clown show in Westminster has obscured what Rutter calls a 'culture of amateurism and irresponsibility', which in turn has created a vicious circle, allowing ministers to justify their contemptuous treatment of the 'blob'.

It is a vicious circle that needs to be broken if the damage caused by Brexit is to be repaired. The Labour Party's proposals for an independent Integrity and Ethics Commission to investigate alleged breaches of the ministerial code would be a start in restoring dwindling public confidence in the integrity of politics. Boris Johnson saw two of his own ethics advisers resign when he was in office. But a new government could potentially consider going further and seek to put the civil service on a new legal footing that would add transparency and accountability. One idea proposed by the Institute for Government would be to mediate the relationship between civil servants and ministers via a newly strengthened Civil Service Board made up from senior politicians, the head of the civil service and non-executive figures appointed on seven- to ten-year terms in a bid to inculcate longer-term thinking.

The attractiveness of such an arrangement would be that it cuts both ways: it would provide a forum to allow ministers to hold the civil service to account for its failures, but create a duty on civil servants to manage the long-term capability of the state in the public interest. The retrospective publication of policy advice, as happens in New Zealand, would force civil servants to raise their game, but also make it harder for ministers to justify cavalierly ignoring that advice. Whatever the precise system, putting the civil service on a statutory footing could ultimately improve the quality of government – not unlike Labour's decision when it came to power in 1997 to grant independence to the Bank of England, or George Osborne's decision to set up the Office for Budget Responsibility in 2010 which, as Liz Truss discovered, is now ignored at a prime minister's peril.

In the end, it's the Brexit cover-up that has sapped public confidence in the project. The desperation to demonstrate the 'benefits of Brexit' has put enormous stress on the system of government, with the resulting spectacle tarnishing the UK's long-standing reputation for sound governance and the rule of law. The politicians who advocated Brexit wildly exaggerated what it could deliver for the UK. The process of defending Brexit has driven British politics into the political upside down, where a Conservative prime minister can build back barriers to trade for all the world to see, while simultaneously claiming to liberalise them. Repairing that damage can only start by a return to industrial and regulatory policies that are based on facts, not fallacy.

4

Buccaneering Britain

Part of the popular allure of Brexit was the notion of a new 'global Britain', a concept that was never precisely defined, but appealed to deep-seated British nostalgia for the days of empire when Britannia was a great maritime force. That was why, in February 2020, Boris Johnson chose the Royal Naval College in Greenwich as the venue for his first major speech setting out the UK's ambition to be a post-Brexit trade power. Inviting his audience to raise their eyes to the ceiling, Johnson picked his way through the baroque masterpiece by James Thornhill which was completed in 1726 as a piece of Royal propaganda and an unapologetic celebration of British naval power. Co-opting Thornhill's work as political prop for the new Brexit era, Johnson marvelled at how the work evoked a moment of 'supreme national self-confidence' for a new British nation following the 1707 Acts of Union which had united the kingdoms of Scotland and England to create the kingdom of Great Britain. 'Free trade is God's diplomacy,' he went on, warming to his theme and quoting the 19th-century champion of free trade Richard Cobden, adding that by voting to leave the EU the UK was now 'leaving its chrysalis' after 'decades of hibernation'.

Johnson acknowledged that, somewhat inconveniently for a nation about to strike out on its own, the global trading environment had become less liberal over the last decade, as the pace of growth in global trade slowed partly thanks to foreign policy differences between Brussels, China and Washington. As Johnson said, global trade had grown at roughly double the rate of global GDP from 1987 to 2007, but was now barely keeping pace. 'The mercantilists are everywhere, the protectionists are gaining ground,' he warned, but said Britain was undeterred and 'ready to take off its Clark Kent spectacles and leap into the phone booth and emerge with its cloak flowing as the supercharged champion, of the right of the populations of the earth to buy and sell freely among each other.'

It was all delivered with a typical Borisian flourish, but as ever the awkward details of the UK's post-Brexit situation were wished away. The fact remains that membership of the EU was also membership of the world's richest and most powerful trading bloc, a single market of 450 million rich-world consumers with a combined GDP of around $17 trillion in 2022. A trading superpower which made the weather in global regulations, in competition with the US. As part of that bloc, the UK had had access to nearly 70 EU-brokered trade agreements which facilitated trade across the planet. Those agreements, which had been signed by Brussels on the UK's behalf, had been obtained using the leverage which came from being a global trading behemoth. After Brexit, go-it-alone Britain, a market of just 55 million people with $3 trillion GDP, would be negotiating trade deals on its own. It was not impossible, but negotiating trade deals is a transactional not sentimental business, as the UK discovered soon after Brexit when it began to convert, or 'roll over', those existing 70 EU-era deals into bilateral deals with old EU trading partners. Even allies were prepared to play hardball, as Canada did in 2019 when it refused to roll over the EU–Canada deal as Johnson flirted with a no-deal exit from the EU. To Downing Street's fury the Canadians waited pretty much until the last minute to see if the UK was going to leave itself in a position where they could get a better deal for free. Welcome to the global trade fight club.

Still, signing new free trade deals was a totemic part of the Brexit prospectus. Vote Leave's campaign literature gave as one of its top reasons for leaving the EU that 'we'll be free to trade with the whole world', adding that the EU 'stops us signing our own trade deals with key allies like Australia and New Zealand, and growing economies like India, China or Brazil'. This was true, narrowly speaking. As a stand-alone country the UK is now free to negotiate its 'own' bilateral trade deals with countries like India, Australia and New Zealand, which (in 2016) the EU had not concluded. Although the EU did conclude a deal with New Zealand in July 2022 and is negotiating a deal with Australia which is due to be concluded in 2023. So while Brexit does leave the UK 'free' to do similar deals, that doesn't necessarily mean it's easy, or indeed that those UK deals, made without the collective bargaining unit of 27 advanced countries, will be better than their EU equivalents.

Taking back control of trade – a policy area which had been subcontracted to Brussels for 40 years – also meant standing up an entirely new Whitehall bureaucracy in order to negotiate those deals. The creation of the Department for International Trade in July 2016, with the Conservative pro-American Liam Fox as the first international trade secretary, was one of Theresa May's first acts as prime minister. But as Fox himself pointed out in a set of controversial remarks soon after taking office, repatriating trade powers from Brussels does not automatically turn the idea of a new, buccaneering Britain into reality. Indeed, as Fox observed, the UK's export performance was actually relatively weak compared to other EU countries, like Germany, which was a global exporting powerhouse driven by a highly efficient, state-backed export promotion machine. Fox got himself into trouble for saying that the UK 'is not the free-trading nation that it once was. We have become too lazy and too fat on our successes in previous generations'. But even if his choice of language was injudicious, he wasn't necessarily wrong. As he concluded: 'What is the point of us reshaping global trade, what is the point of us going out and looking for new markets for the United Kingdom, if we don't have the exporters to fill those markets?'

It is a good question, because unfortunately the immediate effect of Brexit has not been a boom in British exports but a drop in bilateral trade and in the overall number of British companies exporting to the EU. Research by the Centre for Economic Performance at the LSE found that the number of relationships between buyers and sellers tumbled by a third after the introduction of the EU–UK trade deal in January 2021. William Bain, at the British Chambers of Commerce (BCC) said Sampson's findings chimed with reports from smaller businesses that the TCA was making them less competitive. 'Inevitably it is smaller firms which don't have the money, time or logistical capacity to set up within the EU which are being hardest hit. That is also the message from this important study,' he said. Two years after the TCA came into force, those pains were still being felt according to surveys of BCC members. Companies like Doncaster-based Apothecary 87, a small business making premium beard oils and hair balms which was founded in 2012 as the renewed fashion for men's facial hair took hold. The young entrepreneur who started the business, Sam Martin, saw export growth come to a shuddering halt when the TCA came into force on 31 December 2020. 'Before Brexit, our business was 75 per cent exports and the rest in the UK, but Brexit has pretty much turned that number on its head because of the costs and difficulties of getting products to those countries,' he said. The combination of a weaker pound, EU import licences, customs checks and the payment of VAT at the point of import all combined to deter EU customers. In practical terms, that meant that an online customer in the EU that had previously bought a single £10 product from Apothecary was now facing VAT and handling charges that more than doubled or tripled the price, while barber shops in Italy and Spain were forced to obtain cosmetic import licences for up to €1,000 each. As Martin observed: 'Only a true "superfan" of our products could accept these kinds of higher prices.'

Ironically, the smaller businesses suffering lost sales as the result of Brexit red tape are the potential pipeline which should be feeding the future global Britain ambitions that Fox outlined. Restarting that pipeline will be hard if Brexit continues to crimp the supply of future exporters by shrinking the UK's trade with Europe. The non-tariff barriers created by the TCA deter not only EU–UK commerce but also the business investment which drives future trade. The first two full years of UK trade since leaving the EU single market appear to bear out the cost of Brexit's trade-related headwinds. Analysis by Stephen Hunsaker at the UK in a Changing Europe think tank shows that UK total trade volumes started to stagnate in 2016 as uncertainty over the UK's future trading relationship with the EU ate into confidence and investment. Then came the pandemic, which hit trade across the globe, but while the rest of the world bounced back, the UK struggled when compared to other countries in the G20 group of nations. In 2021, the UK experienced only a 2.5 per cent annual growth in trade, placing it last in the G20. These other economies had all suffered the effects of the pandemic, but Brexit was the factor unique to Britain. While it is impossible to completely separate out cause and effect, analysts inferred that the UK's weak performance was the result of that 'Brexit effect'.

The UK trade underperformance has also been particularly acute since the TCA came into force, introducing hurdles to trade with the EU that did not exist when the UK was a member. This despite the fact that a weaker pound after Brexit should, in theory, have increased exports by making UK-made goods and services cheaper when priced in other currencies. But since UK manufacturing is 'intermediate' in nature – i.e. feeds into complex integrated global supply chains – the fall in sterling didn't drive the anticipated uptick in exports because it made the inputs that went into those exports more expensive. In short, Brexit, far from turbo-charging British exporters has – thus far, at least – meant 'global Britain' is doing less trade, not more. In its March 2023 Economic Outlook, the Office for Budget Responsibility estimated that imports would fall by 4 per cent in 2023, while exports would fall by 6.6 per cent, with declines continuing into 2024. The forecast concluded: 'Weak growth in imports and exports over the medium term partly reflect the continuing impact of Brexit.'

Still, Brexit headwinds aside, the newly formed Department for International Trade did break new ground after Brexit, signing bilateral trade deals with Australia in 2021 and New Zealand in 2022. These have been welcomed by business groups like the British Chambers of Commerce, but overall they have equally been clear that the value of these deals cannot offset the costs of leaving the EU single market which is anywhere between 3 per cent and 9 per cent reduction to long-run GDP, depending on how you model the impacts. The UK government's own estimates of the value of the Australia and New Zealand trade deals is tiny, which isn't that surprising given the relative scale of UK trade with these two countries on the other side of the planet. The Australia deal is estimated to be worth 0.08 per cent of additional GDP in 15 years, while the New Zealand deal is put at 0.01 per cent or even, under one scenario, actually a negative 0.01 per cent hit to GDP. So while Boris Johnson hailed the 'fantastic opportunities' provided by the Australia–UK deal – which he said showcased 'global Britain at its best' – those opportunities have to be seen in perspective and weighed against the costs of giving up EU membership.

So too should the UK's post-Brexit ambitions for a broader 'Indo-Pacific tilt', as the foreign secretary put it in September 2022. The UK government joined the Comprehensive and Progressive Agreement for Trans-Pacific Partnership (CPTPP), a free trading bloc of 11 countries in the Indo-Pacific region: Australia, Brunei, Canada, Chile, Japan, Malaysia, Mexico, New Zealand, Peru, Singapore and Vietnam. All of those countries have one thing in common vis-à-vis the UK: they are a very long way away. Trade economists talk about the impact of the 'gravity model' on trade – meaning that the further a country is away from another, the less it trades with that country. Or as the saying goes, 'double the distance, halve the trade'. Even taking into account the impact of the modern digital economy, with the internet making it easier to trade services over long distances via Zoom calls and emails, the reality is that even if Asian markets are growing faster than EU markets, the EU is going to remain the UK's largest trade partner for the foreseeable future. In terms of scale, the CPTPP countries accounted for around 8 per cent of the UK's total trade in 2019, compared to close to 50 per cent for the EU. So even if UK trade with the CPTPP countries continues to grow around 8 per cent a year, as it did in the three years before the Covid-19 pandemic, that's still a relatively small Indo-Pacific pie getting slowly bigger, and a very large EU pie getting relatively smaller.

The UK's own estimates are that CPTPP membership could increase UK GDP by an extra £1.8 billion by 2030 and increase take-home pay by £800 million compared to 2019 levels. Those sound like big numbers, but amount to just 0.08 per cent upside UK GDP, or an average of £24 a head for the UK's 33 million workers. Compare that to calculations by the Resolution Foundation, which has estimated that Brexit, by making the UK economy less open to trade, will see real wages fall by 1.8 per cent, a loss of £470 per worker a year. In the words of the Institute of Directors: 'While flying the flag for "Global Britain" is good for our post-Brexit standing, complete re-orientation is not going to solve the very real problem that businesses currently face, namely that they have many more trade-related challenges than they did six years ago.' In short, as the IoD concluded, the EU–UK relationship, not trade with faraway places in the Pacific, is the 'priority issue' the government needs to address in order to support business.

The fact that the New Zealand trade deal could be potentially negative for UK GDP according to the government's own assessment points to another important reality about the UK's life outside the EU: trade deals always come with trade-offs. This is not something that post-Brexit governments have ever acknowledged, preferring to focus on 'fantastic opportunities', rather than admitting that in any trade deal there are winners and losers. That's true both between the two countries seeking to broker a deal, but also within the competing sectoral interests within those countries. So while the UK–Australia deal might be good for the UK's digital and green technology sectors looking to improve access to Australian markets, that access could have been won at the expense, say, of British farmers. The political challenge is that while FTAs might bring diffuse benefits for the entire economy, that can be overlooked when concentrated costs land on a single sector. This indeed is exactly what the National Farmers Union (NFU) complained happened with the UK–Australia deal, which they described as 'one-sided', giving Australian farmers too much access to UK markets in exchange for too little. The NFU's fear is that if something happens to cause Australian trade to shift very suddenly – say a regional trade war, or a Chinese invasion of Taiwan – then the quotas agreed in the deal leave the UK market at risk of being swamped by Australian beef and lamb.

That might seem like a distant prospect, but Russia's invasion of Ukraine is a reminder of just how quickly trading environments can change. According to the NFU's trade director Nick Von Westonholz, the Australia deal leaves the UK government 'almost no recourse to managing imports if they start proving harmful to UK farm livelihoods'. That could be dismissed as just British farmers moaning, except that it was also the verdict of George Eustice, the Conservative agriculture minister who was in power when the UK–Australia deal was done. In his opinion, as he told MPs, the deal 'gave away far too much for far too little in return' with UK negotiators handing Australia access to UK markets that was 'nearly double what we got in return'. Johnson was accused by his critics – including Eustice, his own former minister – of rushing to secure a deal at any cost, selling the UK short and setting a worrying precedent for future trade negotiations by sending the signal that the UK was desperate for deals in order to demonstrate the 'benefits of Brexit' back home. The UK let itself be seen as a soft touch.

The row over the Australia deal points to a second element of post-Brexit trade negotiations: they are intensely political. During the period of the UK's EU membership, trade deals went largely unnoticed by the general public, and if they did flare up into a political row – as the failed negotiations for a US–EU deal did in 2016 – then British ministers could always blame the EU for getting it wrong. Not any more. If the UK is going to conclude a trade deal with the US, for example, it will have to negotiate the often intense political feelings thrown up by contentious issues such as whether to accept chlorine-washed chicken or hormone-injected beef. The Australia deal has already inflamed passions, with an NFU petition to defend British food standards attracting over a million signatures after it was backed by celebrity chefs including Jamie Oliver and Delia Smith. Trade creates a tangle of political contradictions: the constituency that is passionate about the prospects of 'buccaneering Britain' and cheaper food can be equally passionate about defending British beef or lamb farmers, or expecting high animal welfare standards.

And the British public are sensitive when it comes to animals. Post-Brexit governments, starting with Boris Johnson in that speech in Greenwich, have repeatedly said that they will not allow UK food and animal welfare standards to slip. But fair trade campaigners and farming groups say the government is choosing its words very carefully; because if the UK signs a trade deal that allows products made with lower environmental, labour and animal welfare standards to freely enter the UK, then it is effect-ively 'importing' those lower standards. These issues can become subjects of popular concern, from palm oil plantations destroying rainforest to pollution from shrimp farms and sugar cane planta-tions choking rivers and killing coral reefs. UK producers held to higher domestic standards, find themselves at a structural competitive disadvantage as imports made to lower standards enter the UK economy and undercut them.

This would become a particularly acute issue in a US–UK trade negotiation. The UK bans the use of so-called 'gestation crates' and growth-enhancing feed additives such as Ractopamine in pig production, both of which are widely used in intensive US farming systems. The gestation crate is a steel cage that holds a sow in place so she doesn't crush her young and is widely considered inhumane, but it does improve productivity and reduce costs. In 2022 only 3 per cent of the entire US pig herd was protected by restrictions on the use of such crates, and only California had a total ban. If the UK does a trade deal with America, then US trade negotiators have made it clear they will demand that the UK accepts US pork, raised to those (lower) standards. That could mean cheaper cuts for UK consumers, but it could cause trouble at home as UK farmers protest at unfair competition and animal welfare campaigners reveal how US pork is produced. It also complicates trade with the EU, where pork raised to those standards is not legal. Brussels will therefore want to be sure that such pork – if it enters the UK market – does not 'leak' into the EU market. That, in turn, entails more stringent checks at the border for UK exporters sending British meat into the EU – a far more important market for agricultural products than the US.

And it's not just issues around food standards and farming that can touch raw political nerves. Modern comprehensive trade agreements touch on many other politically sensitive areas, including environmental protections, human rights and immigration. Negotiations with India were temporarily derailed in October 2022 when the UK home secretary Suella Braverman raised concerns that the deal was going to require the UK to grant too many visa concessions to Indian workers, which she said were the worst group for overstaying their visas already. 'I have concerns about having an open borders migration policy with India because I don't think that's what people voted for with Brexit,' she said in an interview, causing fury in Delhi which promptly ordered a retaliatory go-slow on UK visa applications.

Human rights is another area where trade can get complicated. The UK, when a member of the EU, backed the inclusion of a standard human rights clause in all agreements signed by the bloc. Now free to go its own way, the UK has not included a similar clause in its own deals with Australia and New Zealand, setting a precedent for future deals with countries like India and China. The UK's Integrated Review into future defence, development and foreign policy made repeated references to the desire to promote British 'values', but the absence of a standard human rights clause in post-Brexit trade deals (a clause that deliberately doesn't discriminate between countries) has caused concern among MPs. Parliament's International Trade Committee said the government had 'relinquished an important lever for promoting "British values"' by not including the clauses. The Labour Party has vowed to include such clauses if it wins power in 2024, promising 'strong labour protections and high standards' will be baked into any future deals. Perhaps, but as a small country seeking deals with larger regimes, it may be that the UK simply doesn't have the heft to insist on such clauses. Or it may not want such clauses, if it believes that their absence might help the UK cut deals with countries where the EU cannot, or will not, do the same.

Which points to the most important truth about the UK's post-Brexit trade powers: with newfound power comes newfound responsibility. Trade deals impact multiple areas of life. The texts may be impenetrable, but the consequences are very real. Trade deals can affect everything from what we eat to how our own countryside is used and farmed; they affect immigration policy and the image of the UK abroad. All of which explains why it is important to consult and explain the objectives of such deals at the outset. Governments might baulk at delays caused by scrutiny and oversight, but without obtaining the buy-in of both Parliament and the public, they risk the kind of popular backlash that has derailed major deals in the past, including the EU's attempt to sign a comprehensive deal with the US. The row over how farmers were sold short in the UK–Australia deal was a flash in the pan compared the fights that will erupt if the communications and consultation around any future UK–US trade deal are not handled properly.

But as things stand, the UK has some of the weakest controls over deal-making in the world. Parliament, unlike the US Congress, has no legal right to be informed of the negotiating mandate or ratify its contents. During negotiations, MPs and parliamentary committees have no right to access documents relating to the deal (unlike the US Congress and the European Parliament). And in contrast to the Biden administration's worker-centred trade policy, which is based on the idea that governments get better deals when their workers are consulted, the UK government explicitly does not consult UK labour unions over the shape of trade deals. And even once deals are done, the UK Parliament is not required to ratify the deal, but can only delay it once the completed treaty is formally laid before the House. In practice, when the Australia deal was done, the Commons was, in the words of one MP, 'asked to pass bare-bones legislation, implementing an agreement that we have not been given the opportunity to scrutinise'. As Emily Jones, Associate Professor of Public Policy at Oxford University's Blavatnik School of Government, put it: 'Unless changes are made, the UK's future trade deals will receive less scrutiny than the trade deals it entered as part of the EU.' So as things stands, for all the claims that Brexit would re-empower the UK's sovereign parliament, post-Brexit governments, in their haste to complete trade deals, have created a system that is far less open and democratic than the one enjoyed under EU membership.

5

Industrial Revolutions

It is not surprising that Brexit provided an economic shock to the British economy. Upending a trading relationship that had become deeply entwined over more than 40 years was never going to be without costs. But those who believed it could ultimately lead to better things for the UK argued that even if plunging into the icy waters of independence from Brussels was painful at first, over time it would prove an invigorating tonic for Britain's economy. (A reversal of the 'cold shower of competition' which advocates for EU membership advanced in the 1970s.) Brexiters reasoned that once businesses that traded with Europe had adjusted to the same level of form-filling as businesses that traded with the rest of the world, then more UK companies would be 'export-fit' and able to tap into the faster-growing markets of the Asia-Pacific region. It was a seductive narrative, but one that overlooked just how enmeshed UK exporters had become in European trade, and how negative the impacts of Brexit would be, not just for EU trade, but across the board.

Based on the performance of UK trade so far, the 'short, sharp shock' theory of Brexit is looking wildly optimistic. Part of the underlying problem, according to research conducted by economists from the Bank of England, is that Brexit is not like other post-war 'uncertainty shocks'. When business was hit by events like the 1970s oil price shock, the 9/11 attacks or the collapse of Lehman Brothers in 2008, it was buffeted for a time, but then managed to stabilise and adjust to the new reality. The immediate impact of these types of crises was, relatively speaking, short-lived. Brexit presents a much deeper structural challenge, or what the economists called a 'large, broad and long-lasting increase in uncertainty'. So while trade agreements create certainty among traders, leaving the EU single market was, in effect, a 'reverse' trade deal. As a result it has had the opposite effect, leaving both international and domestic investors unsure whether the UK is a good bet for the future.

The persistent uncertainty caused by Brexit is illustrated by the fact that even after the TCA was signed, the investment outlook did not improve. In September 2019, just before the TCA was finally agreed, the Bank of England identified three areas of uncertainty for business: the shape of the UK's future relationship with the EU, access to migrant labour and UK product regulations. But nearly three years after the deal came into force, the UK regulatory environment, which is so important for business, is still in many respects up in the air. That's partly thanks to the Retained EU Law Bill which threatened to review or revoke all EU-derived law by the end of 2023, but also because of delays to the introduction in the UK of new regulatory regimes covering everything from chemicals to construction products and medical devices. That means more uncertainty. As for the trade deal David Frost brokered, the opposition Labour Party has promised to change and improve the deal if it wins power. A general election looms before the end of 2024. No one knows exactly what they might be able to negotiate with Brussels. More uncertainty.

Brexit allowed the British state to 'take back control', but the downside of repatriating rule-making powers to London is that it creates a permanent and structural climate of uncertainty for business. Industry may have often complained about the cost and bureaucracy of EU regulation but it came dependably down the bureaucratic pipeline and, once complied with, opened the door to a market eight times the size of the UK's. Since taking back control from Brussels at the 2016 referendum, the UK has so far piloted the post-Brexit economy erratically and unpredictably. But even with a more sober leader at the helm, like Rishi Sunak, Brexit still inevitably leads to a constant regulatory instability in the UK's relationship with Europe. The UK is like a regulatory iceberg that has been calved off the EU's continental ice sheet. The two systems, which were once of a piece, have separated and are drifting apart. So even if the UK stands still, the EU is slowly moving away.

Managing this so-called 'passive divergence' between the UK and the EU takes time, money and bandwidth, both in the UK's boardrooms and in Whitehall. Take one small example: the EU announced that from February 2024 it was upgrading emissions testing standards for new cars and vans from the current 'Euro 6d' standard to a stricter 'Euro 6e' regime. Unfortunately, the post-Brexit UK rules required new vehicles to be tested to the 'Euro 6d' standard before being allowed on British roads. This created the crazy situation that a vehicle tested to a higher '6e' standard in the EU would not be deemed to have met the lower '6d' standard required in the UK. As the Department for Transport admitted: 'EU Euro 6e approval cannot be accepted as demonstration of compliance with the current Euro 6d requirements, which apply under the GB approval scheme.' This was obviously a bureaucratic absurdity and the UK government promised to revise the GB rules accordingly, but such processes take time and effort, both for manufacturers and for government departments in Whitehall – which is just bureaucratic pain for no economic gain.

As the Bank of England study noted, it looks as if the permanent uncertainty of Brexit saps resources and undermines investment. The impact on business investment, which is vital to growth in the productivity and output of the UK economy, has been clear. It flatlined after 2016 but, even after the TCA was signed in 2020, did not recover. Even allowing for the impacts of the Covid-19 pandemic, which temporarily spooked investment in the US and the EU, the UK undershot those trends to the tune of £60 billion a year. As Carl Ennis, the UK boss of the global industrial technology giant Siemens observed, given all the uncertainty that still surrounds the UK trading environment, it has proved difficult to get global boardrooms to commit money to the UK when they have options to go elsewhere: 'What's really missing in the UK is stability,' he said nearly two years after the TCA came into force. 'We have seen it is much more difficult to attract capital to the UK – and that's across industry in general.'

Business is not 'getting the hang' of Brexit because it creates permanent barriers to trade. Take a company like LMK Thermosafe Ltd, a small business based in Suffolk that produces industrial heaters for drums and containers which are used by some of the world's biggest companies including Unilever,

AstraZeneca, Procter & Gamble and Rentokil. Its products have been supplied to over 70 countries since 1985, but at the time of Brexit over 30 per cent of its exports went to the EU. After Brexit, the boss of the company, Mark Newton, hired an extra staff member to deal with Brexit bureaucracy in the belief that after a period of adjustment business would continue as normal. But it didn't.

Indeed after two full years of trading with the EU under the terms of the TCA, Newton was forced to do as Kiran Tawadey from Hampstead Tea did, and take space in a Dutch warehousing operation in order to smooth his export operations to Europe. The combination of customs paperwork, 27 different VAT regimes and proving his products complied with EU technical standards all aggregated to make delivery of his products marginally unreliable. 'I had been hoping to avoid it, I thought we could get the border processes down pat, but I've had to accept it. It all adds cost and subtracts from the margin, employing a Dutch warehouse, fiscal representative [to manage VAT issues] and so on.'

What Newton discovered was even having taken on an extra staff member to handle the paperwork, and even when the paperwork was done properly, Brexit created a layer of uncertainty. 'Some things just go wrong, even when you get it all right,' he says. It might just be EU officials being difficult, picky about the formalities, or a single line error on a form, but that can result in products getting delayed. It's not that Brexit stops Newton from exporting his products tariff-free, it just makes it sufficiently more difficult to grow his business in Europe. The disadvantage might be marginal, but when your competitor is operating inside the single market with no bureaucratic frictions at all, that gives them a competitive advantage. This is why, looking to the future, it is by no means certain that familiarity with the system will see this negative impact of Brexit diminish over time. In fact, at the point of Brexit, companies like Thermosafe had a 'stock' of existing relationships in which both sides had invested over many years. These didn't disappear overnight, and so business persisted despite the barriers. The outlook for the future is less certain. According to Newton: 'The regulations and paperwork for Europe is most definitely an inhibitor for growth, most definitely.'

The question is whether the barriers to trade caused by Brexit will make it harder to grow business in the future – to forge the next generation of relationships for businesses like LMK Thermosafe. 'It's definitely an ongoing drama,' says Newton. 'Blue-chip clients have stuck with us, but with our EU competitors they are definitely sabre-rattling with our distributors, saying, "You don't want to do business with the Brits, it's all just too complicated."' This is an experience that has been echoed widely across industry. A survey of 580 businesses by the Institute of Directors published in March 2023 found that the majority now feel 'at a disadvantage' to EU companies who can provide goods or services 'often more quickly, sometimes more cheaply, and without the hassle of paperwork'. As one cleaning services small business explained: 'Our Irish customers now will buy the material off a mainland EU mill or distributor and have the material sent to our competitors in Germany or Holland to minimise all the horrible red tape and tariff issues etc. that Brexit has caused. There is no way we can influence their return to our company because it just causes more work and costs for them.'

There are already signs that this is having an impact. Analysis by Aston Business School of post-Brexit trade data showed a sharp fall in the varieties of goods traded between the EU and UK, dropping to 42,000 from 70,000 before the new rules came into effect. According to Professor Jun Du, who conducted the research, smaller companies have been hardest hit because the barriers are a more significant cost relative to the value of trade. This bodes ill for the future because, simply put, today's small firms are tomorrow's bigger ones. 'That's why we are worried about future growth,' she said. 'When you lose that, your pipeline breaks.' And the pipeline is important, because while UK manufacturing accounts for only 10 per cent of the UK economy, according to a 2020 Cambridge University report for the Business Department it has a disproportionately high share of UK exports, at 49 per cent. Manufacturing is also a significant driver of research and development spending in the private sector and provides higher-value jobs. Wages in manufacturing are about 15 per cent above the national average. And when it comes to modern manufacturing, the UK is not an island. British manufacturers make very few things from start to finish, but play a role in highly complex and interwoven EU supply chains. In fact, around 65 per cent of the UK's exports to the EU take the form of 'intermediate' inputs into finished goods and services, according to the Institute for Fiscal Studies.

Those products – a German machine tool, say, containing British-made parts – are also often exported onwards to the same fast-growing markets that the architects of 'global Britain' say the UK should be targeting. But Brexit border frictions now gum up those supply chains. And reduced access to the EU indirectly reduces the ability of UK manufacturers to export to non-EU markets as well. This uncertainty can be seen in trade surveys conducted by UK manufacturing bodies that show EU companies are increasingly nervous of trading with the UK. A members' survey by Make UK, the manufacturers' trade lobby, in March 2023 found that over one-third of all UK manufacturing inputs came via Europe but almost half of the manufacturers (48 per cent) said that EU suppliers were cautious about supplying to UK customers. Worryingly, almost 20 per cent of manufacturers reported that they have reduced the number of suppliers from the EU in the last 12 months, a clear sign that vital neighbourhood trading relationships are atrophying as a result of Brexit. These findings also chime with the sharp downturn in EU exports to the UK since Brexit.

How Brexit became Certifiable

One area that has caused needless headaches and heartache for British business after Brexit has been the issue of product certification. There are myriad technical rules that regulate the products we all commonly buy and sell. They cover inputs into the electronics, manufacturing and construction industries – everything from specialist adhesives to airbags for cars or gearboxes for passenger lifts; all these things require certification in order to be placed on the market as part of those highly integrated EU supply chains already described. The EU has a system for showing that these goods conform with European health, safety and environmental protection standards – the 'CE' mark. Look on the back of any electronic or household device and you will see one, offering a guarantee the product has been made to the correct standard. After Brexit, the UK government under Boris Johnson wanted to make a clean break from the EU's regulatory systems. The idea was that by being free to diverge, particularly on future generations of products like medical devices, a nimbler UK would be able to glean an advantage over their European competitors. To this end the UK announced it would introduce a rival 'UKCA' mark – standing for 'UK Conformity Assessed' – which all UK and EU companies would be required to use when selling or making products in the UK.

This appealed to the Brexiters' red tape fantasy, but for business it was a nightmare. For the vast majority of existing products the UK has agreed that it won't have a different standard than the EU. If a company had a 'CE' mark for its radiators that certified it safe for sale in 27 EU countries, what was the point of a 'UKCA' mark just to sell in the UK? This was particularly irksome since the UK had decided to remain part of the EU's European Committee on Standardisation 'CEN' and 'CENELEC', the bodies that set Europe-wide standards for industrial and electrical goods. British industry, which uses components drawn from all over the EU, gained nothing by putting a British-only badge on a product that already conforms to an EU standard. As Stephen Phipson, the chief executive of Make UK said, it 'only adds costs and extra bureaucracy'. More pain, for no gain. And the UKCA mark doesn't just impact UK companies. It also hits EU companies that export to the UK. Given the size of the UK market and the hassle involved in obtaining a UKCA mark it is not difficult to see why EU and Asian exporters would either scale back on the number of products they sell to the UK market, or even to give up on selling to the UK market altogether. That means less choices for UK industry and consumers and less flexibility when participating in neighbourhood supply chains.

Which is why British industry has waged a persistent campaign to get the government to drop the UKCA mark where standards remain aligned. In boardrooms the UKCA mark has come to symbolise the Brexiters' dogmatic pursuit of divergence in the face of commercial realities. Another membership survey by Make UK found that three-quarters of respondents wanted the UK to continue to recognise CE-marked goods. The UKCA scheme also exposed a key truth about divergence: that any potential upside of adopting a different standard has to be weighed against the downside costs of implementing the new regime. Because a UKCA mark is not just a sticker or a label that can be slapped on a product. A company, for example, that makes passenger lifts for sale all over Europe will find itself having to re-certify components in the UK. And even if the standards are identical, for a safety-critical product like a lift, the manufacturer would still need to find a qualified certification body in the UK to run the tests needed to obtain the UKCA certificate. But given the sheer volume of products that need certifying, it has become clear that there is not sufficient testing capacity in the UK to meet industry demand.

And so gravity and reality have taken over. The UKCA scheme that was originally due to start in January 2022 has now been pushed back to January 2025. The lack of testing capacity in the UK (which before Brexit was part of an EU-wide system) forced the government's hand. Car companies couldn't find the pyrotechnics labs to certify the airbags for their cars. Building companies couldn't find bodies to test basic house-building products. The UK Construction Leadership Council warned that inability to certify radiators in the UK, for instance, could delay the construction of over 150,000 homes in a single year. It was calculated that since the UK only had one testing facility for radiators, it would in theory take 75 years to retest them all. That is obviously an absurd calculation but it illustrates a point, that in a broad swathe of everyday commerce regulatory divergence creates cost. It also brings more uncertainty as the government constantly shifts the deadline in the face of reality – three times already since the policy was announced.

For now, UK companies can still use CE-marked goods, but as Peter Caplehorn of the Construction Products Association observed, the current patched-up arrangements are likely to 'limit innovation' and the introduction of new products the UK because the market is just too small for many EU and global companies to bother registering products for the UK separately. For businesses like LMK Thermosafe that spent 'tens of thousands' of pounds gearing up to comply with the new paperwork, successive delays have effectively penalised them for preparing to implement UKCA while rewarding businesses that didn't bother. And without clarity from the government, the uncertainty continues to loom, because the current halfway house allowing companies to continue using the EU's CE system doesn't incentivise companies to invest in UK compliance, which in turn doesn't drive an expansion in UK testing facilities.

Which is why the British Chambers of Commerce (BCC) wants the entire scheme delayed to 2026, to give time for a long-term solution to be negotiated to avoid extra costs for both importing and exporting businesses. As the BCC's head of trade policy William Bain put it, 'Ultimately we also need a system that will avoid any unnecessary future cliff-edges.' There is a bitter irony in all this. During the Brexit negotiation the EU said that it would not allow the UK to become a 'certification hub' off the coast of Europe, but the net result of the current stop-gap arrangement is that the exact reverse has happened. The UK is unilaterally recognising the EU's CE-marked goods, turning the EU into a certification hub for the UK. Another area where the UK hasn't taken back control.

A Lack of Post-Brexit Chemistry

The chemical industry has a similar story to tell. While it might not have the headline-grabbing potential of cars or fashion, chemicals are integral to almost everything we consume, from car paints to haircare products, plastics to pesticides. The industry is also a valuable manufacturing sector for the UK, supporting over 3,500 companies and half a million high-value jobs, accounting for 9 per cent of total UK goods exports, worth £50 billion in 2019. Well over half of these exports went to EU Member states. Before Brexit, all chemicals used in the EU had to be registered in a vast database held by the European Chemicals Agency (ECHA) based in Helsinki. The 'Registration, Evaluation, Authorisation and Restriction of Chemicals' – or 'EU REACH' for short – came into force in 2007 in order to harmonise a large number of different EU chemicals regulations in a single place.

During the years of EU membership, it cost British-based companies some £500 million to populate that database, carrying out expensive tests and collecting troves of data in order to win approval to place individual chemicals on the market. But because associate membership of ECHA would have required the UK to accept the writ of the European Court of Justice – which crossed Frost and Johnson's red lines – it was ruled out. The result? A decision to build another copycat British system – the 'UK REACH' database which, at the government's own last estimate, will cost the industry around £2 billion to populate with data that is already sitting in Helsinki. That works out at an average of £91,000 for each of the 22,400 individual substances that has been registered with the UK database. Not surprisingly the chemical industry has urged the government to rethink such a scheme, since it duplicates work they have already done in the EU. The deadline to complete registrations has been pushed back to at least October 2026, with some substances being pushed out to 2028 and 2030.

For Dani Loughran, the managing director of Aston Chemicals, a medium-sized cosmetics chemicals company in Bucking-hamshire, registering for UK REACH will cost the same as for EU REACH, but will still only grant access to the UK market. Similarly Adrian Hanrahan, the boss of Robinson Brothers Ltd, a speciality chemicals company based in West Bromwich, said that UK REACH was costing him £155,000 a year – for nothing. And these costs relate only to the existing 'stock' of chemical registrations, it doesn't speak to the uncertainty that UK REACH is causing when it comes to placing new chemicals on the UK market, and what that is doing to future trade with the EU. The Chemical Industries Association trade body has warned that the ongoing lack of clarity over requirements for registering new chemicals in the UK is deterring companies from importing EU-registered chemicals into Great Britain. Robinson Brothers says that one large German company for which they do product development work has recently stripped any UK-based businesses from getting new projects, with all the work being placed within Germany and France. 'We and another UK company missed out,' Hanrahan said. 'And you can understand it. Why would you start development work in the UK, with all the uncertainty over UK REACH, when you get certainty from EU REACH?'

Hanrahan and Loughran's frustrations point to a truth about Brexit that is often not fully appreciated: that while the stock of existing relationships (in which investment had already been sunk at the point of Brexit) may have endured, the future flow of investments is at ongoing risk from UK divergence and supply-chain frictions. Which is to say, companies don't necessarily just get used to the border frictions as a one-off cost, and then move on. Those frictions risk crimping future growth and investment plans. This is why bosses like Loughran and Hanrahan cannot contain their frustration when Brexiters like Jacob Rees-Mogg say that UK REACH is going to make the UK nimbler and more competitive. 'It reduces prices in this country and makes the UK economy more competitive,' Rees-Mogg told the BBC in January 2023. But Loughran says the reverse is the case: 'UK REACH is actually likely to lead to fewer chemicals available in the UK, and hence less competition,' she says. 'It is also likely to be the biggest, richest companies that can afford to pay for UK REACH, so it also disadvantages UK small businesses and gives an unfair advantage to multinational corporations.'

According to Brexiter logic, now that it is outside the EU, the UK should be able to steal a march on the sclerotic EU system, driving competitiveness and lowering barriers to entry into the marketplace for smaller companies. But that fails to understand the David and Goliath situation that the UK now finds itself in. Even if the UK companies don't like the EU regulation, it makes sense for them to follow the rules, and accept oversight of the EU's court, in order to gain access to the EU single market. At the same time, the government has simply struggled to build the bureaucratic capacity to deliver its own bespoke regime. That isn't all that surprising. The EU regulator in Helsinki employs 600 people with an annual budget of €110 million, compared with the £13 million a year budgeted for the UK version, including up to 50 staff. At the same time, environmental and conservation groups have raised concerns that the UK is adopting a lighter-touch approach to some hazardous substances, an approach that risks undermining public confidence in an industry that requires the maintenance of public trust. That is why the Chemical Industries Association has repeatedly said that it does not want to see a bonfire of regulation.

Autos: A Brexit Breakdown

As for the UK car industry – a 'cornerstone' industry of British manufacturing – Brexit has piled obstacles in the way of an industry that was riding high at the time of the Brexit referendum. That year the UK made 1.7 million cars, with the industry bullishly predicting it would pass the 2 million mark in 2017 for the first time since the 1970s. By 2022 production had plummeted to 775,000 units – the worst performance since 1956. There were short-term factors at play – the war in Ukraine halted Russian exports and a global shortage of microchips paused some production lines – but Brexit has also created potentially fatal longer-term headwinds for an industry that exports half its production to the EU. Big brands like Nissan and Toyota are well known to the public, but less visible is the network of smaller companies that support their factories via supply chains that criss-cross the EU. Those companies now face all non-tariff barriers, making them less reliable and more expensive than their European competitors. Nissan bosses warned in February 2023 that unless the UK could remain competitive with other countries on subsidies and supply chains, there was no guarantee that it would make the new electric models of its Juke and Qashqai cars in the UK. The clock is starting to tick on addressing these issues, either smoothing relations with the EU or rebuilding the UK auto supply chain which has dwindled in recent years.

But British-based car makers have a more existential problem than border frictions, costly though these are. Although the EU–UK trade deal is often described as 'zero-tariff', that doesn't mean everything in the UK automatically goes into the EU without paying tariffs. To win that privilege, goods must be deemed sufficiently 'made in the UK', otherwise companies could just import cheap goods from Asia, say, and send them on into Europe tariff-free, undercutting EU manufacturers who are protected by the EU's common external tariff. That's why trade deals have so-called 'rules of origin' which mean that exporters have to prove that their goods are sufficiently home-made to enter the EU single market without paying duties. Typically a product needs to contain around 50 per cent 'originating content' or the importer must pay tariffs – in the case of a finished car the tariff is 10 per cent. For car brands looking to build cars in the UK, a 10 per cent tariff on exports to Europe would make the mass-production of vehicles in the UK uneconomic.

The challenge for UK-based car makers is how to continue meeting that 'made in UK' threshold in the era of electric vehicles. Well over one-third of the value of any electric car is made up by the battery, so unless those batteries are made in the UK, there is no way a British-made car will qualify for zero-tariff export to the EU. When the UK signed the trade deal it negotiated a brief holiday from the requirement to hit a 55 per cent local-made threshold, but from 2024 the requirement for UK-made content will slowly start to ratchet up. The EU also refused to allow the UK to count parts imported from other EU trade partners like Japan as 'local content', increasing the pressure on the UK to develop its own battery-making capacity. The UK industry has already quietly asked for an extension to the deadline once, but was rebuffed by the European Commission in December 2022. There is still time before 2024 for the EU to change tack and relax the deadlines, but fundamentally the trade deal is designed to squeeze the UK and make it more attractive for car makers to set up in the EU. The pressure is already starting to tell. In May, the car maker Stellantis, which owns Vauxhall, warned the British government that unless the current rules of origin 'holiday' for electric vehicles could be extended until 2027 it might have to close its electric van factory at Ellesmere Port in Cheshire where it had planned to make vehicles for both UK and EU markets.

Bearing in mind the importance of a dash for UK battery making, the bad news is that the UK is falling far behind the EU when it comes to building the large-scale battery plants – so-called 'gigafactories' – that are essential to the viability of any future for the UK car industry. UK investment in battery plants stalled after 2016 as uncertainty clouded the horizon, but while the UK was arguing with itself over Brexit, the EU was forging ahead. Seven EU member states have combined to create a €20 billion European Battery Alliance to drive the creation of EU battery supply chains. By the start of 2023, there were at least 40 gigafactories up and running or under construction in the EU compared to one in the UK – the Nissan factory in Sunderland. When a second battery plant at Nissan comes online in 2025 its 12GWh capacity will be enough for 100,000 cars a year.

It's a very small start in an industry that so recently aspired to make 2 million cars a year. Globally the automotive industry will spend over a trillion dollars by the end of this decade in the transition to electric. By contrast, the UK has earmarked £800 million, which is a drop in the ocean compared to the subsidies being offered in the EU and the US. As a member of the EU, the UK could have been part of the European Battery Alliance; it could also have drawn on capital from the European Investment Bank, which it was forced to leave at the point of Brexit. At that time the European Investment Bank was providing about £5 billion a year to UK projects, with a heavy skew towards green technology.

EU state subsidies for batteries and green technologies, which are being expanded in 2023 as part of the EU's Green Deal Industrial Plan, have been dwarfed by those offered by Joe Biden's administration. The $369 billion Inflation Reduction Act includes deep subsidies on battery plant production that are guaranteed right up until the 2030s, offering long-term certainty to investors. And even if the UK government could find the cash, the UK market alone is not big enough to build companies of sufficient scale to be viable. The UK is therefore overshadowed by both its neighbours, playing piggy-in-the-middle to an EU–US subsidy war which it cannot possibly win. What is more, it is not at all clear whether the UK government has any kind of strategy to compete.

So while successive post-Brexit British governments have talked a good game about a 'green industrial revolution', the UK is inexorably falling behind. The collapse of the £3.8 billion British-volt gigafactory project in Blyth, Northumberland, in January 2023 – only a year after Boris Johnson hailed it as a 'major boost' for British industry – was a salutary reminder of how exposed the UK car industry has been left by Brexit. Britishvolt was badly managed and oversold its technology, but ultimately failed because it didn't have any major customers on the horizon who would guarantee to buy its batteries. In 2019 Tesla opted to build its cars in Berlin, with Elon Musk citing Brexit uncertainty as one reason for the decision. Honda stopped manufacturing in the UK in 2021 while BMW announced in October 2022 it was shifting some production of the electric Mini to China. Toyota has still given no indication of how the UK will fit into its long-term EV strategy. Ultimately the future of the industry will only be secured if the battery conundrum can be solved, and that will mean the UK finding a way to compete against the massive industrial and energy subsidies, alongside planning easements, now being handed out by the US and the EU in order to attract investment. As David Bailey, professor of business economics at the Birmingham Business School, put it: 'The race for EV battery making is well underway, and the UK is barely off the starting grid.'

The challenges facing British industry are complex. Brexit is only one piece of the puzzle, but it is a piece that is unique to the UK. Microchip shortages, fierce competition for skilled workers and sky-rocketing energy prices after the break-out of war in the Ukraine are challenges being faced by many of the UK's competitors too. Which is why it is so concerning that UK exports, investment and productivity are underperforming competitor economies. The OBR noted in its March 2023 assessment of the UK economy that while all major advanced economies saw trade collapse during the pandemic, the UK had not recovered at anything like the same speed as other G7 economies. By the third quarter of 2022, G7 trade volumes were on average 5.5 per cent above 2019 levels, but the UK's were still 3 per cent below. Brexit, which will not be reversed in the foreseeable future, provides additional headwinds that make it tougher to face many of those challenges. Industry CEOs are clear that in areas like car making and chemical manufacturing, where supply chains are deeply enmeshed in the fabric of Europe, divergence on regulations – for example with UK REACH and the UKCA mark – just creates unwanted cost and complexity. Even where there are potential benefits to divergence, the government has struggled, administratively, to build the regulatory apparatus that would in theory deliver them. Many of these problems arise directly from the choices the Boris Johnson government made in negotiating such a low-ambition trade deal with the EU. Other countries on the EU's periphery, like Switzerland or Norway, have much closer relationships and still consider themselves 'sovereign' countries.

The social and political impacts of policies that undermine UK industry are also worth considering more broadly. Manufacturing is key to the prosperity of the regional economies of the Midlands and the North that Boris Johnson promised to 'level up' as part of his pledge to close the UK's north–south divide. In those areas, manufacturing provides a disproportionate number of the higher-quality, higher-productivity jobs that pay

better and bring more value to the local economy. Although
overall manufacturing accounts for less than 10 per cent of the
UK economy, in the Midlands and the North manufacturing
accounts for 15 to 17 per cent of the local economy. Those
areas were also among those, like Sunderland, that voted most
enthusiastically for Brexit even though the North East was the
only UK region with a manufacturing trade surplus with the
EU pre-Brexit.

Indeed, in many of the so-called 'Red Wall' marginal constit-
uencies that Boris Johnson turned Tory blue in the December
2019 general election, the number of manufacturing jobs
outstrips the size of the Conservative electoral majority by two,
three or four times. In the most extreme case, the seat of Bury
North in Greater Manchester, the number of manufacturing
jobs is 40 times bigger than the political majority. These were
the same places that were told that Brexit would deliver more
money for the NHS and a resurgence for UK trade as 'global
Britain' was given fresh wings outside the EU. That isn't what
has happened. Exports have fallen, as has the UK's overall openness to trade. On the doorsteps it's hard to imagine that many
voters cared or even knew about 'UKCA' marks or the complex-
ities of 'UK REACH', or ever saw such things as a vital badge
of sovereignty. Brexit was sold as a programme to set British
industry free; but for a huge number of companies all it's done
is gum up the pipes of trade. As the former Siemens boss Juergen
Maier put it, since leaving the EU, 'we've got red tape coming
out of our earholes'. He called on Britain's politicians to begin
an 'an honest, decent conversation about alignment of regulation
and about being close to the single market and having proper
"frictionless access", like we were promised originally'.

6

Immigration and the Business of People

When would-be Leave voters were asked by the British Election Study in April 2016 for a single word to sum up why they wanted to leave the EU, there was one that stood out far beyond any other: immigration. In the resultant word cloud that was generated to illustrate the motivation of Leavers, immigration dwarfed all the other key words, including 'control', 'sovereignty' and 'borders'. By contrast, Remain voters' focus was overwhelmingly on 'economy' followed by 'trade', 'security' and 'rights'. The political debate over immigration became increasingly toxic after the 2004 enlargement of the EU when several eastern European countries and the trio of Baltic states joined the bloc. A sharp rise in the amount of EU migration to the UK followed. In the year running up to the 2016 referendum the immigration issue was given renewed impetus by the migrant crisis which engulfed Europe in the summer of 2015. Hundreds of thousands of refugees fleeing the Syrian civil war crossed the Mediterranean and Aegean seas and travelled onwards into northern Europe via Greece, Hungary and Italy, with some ending up in encampments outside Calais. While EU countries, led by Germany, gave homes to the bulk of these people, politicians in the UK stoked concerns over the threat posed by this exodus from the Middle East. David Cameron spoke of a 'swarm of people coming across the Mediterranean' during a television interview, using language usually reserved for insects. The infamous Nigel Farage 'Breaking Point' poster during the 2016 campaign also blurred the refugee crisis with Brexiters' promise to end EU free movement and 'take back control' of UK borders.

Those refugees from war were, of course, an entirely different category of people from the EU citizens who had exercised their single market free movement rights to live and work in Britain during the period of the UK's membership of the EU. The arrival of large numbers of EU workers after 2004 was accompanied by an increase in the numbers of UK voters saying that immigration was a major concern. By the time Brexit actually occurred in 2020 about 5.5 million EU citizens were living in the UK and eligible to apply for 'settled status' to remain living in the country. Something that was almost always lost in the popular debate was that those EU workers, many from eastern European countries like Hungary and Poland, were significant net contributors to the UK's public finances. EU migrants who arrived in the UK in 2016 would make a net positive contribution to Treasury coffers of more than £19 billion over the lifetime of their stay in the UK, according to a 2018 study by the consultancy Oxford Economics. And comparatively speaking they were more productive than those already living in the UK, contributing approximately £2,300 more to UK public finances in 2016–17 than the average UK-based adult. Not that you would have known that from reading the conser-vative sections of the British press or listening to much of the political debate over immigration.

Still, if anything was clear about Brexit it was that it was a vote to end free movement of people. In its place the govern-ment introduced a 'points-based' system which ended prefer-ential treatment for Europeans: the same immigration rules applied to everyone, wherever they came from in the world. Polls continue to show majority public support for this approach. Under the new system higher-skilled workers with jobs earning over £26,200 (or above the 'going rate' for their industry) can apply for a skilled worker visa. A small number of jobs where the UK has a lack of workers are included on the Shortage Occupations List (SOL) where the barriers to enter the UK are lowered, including reducing the required salary for a visa. Because, by its nature, 'free' movement didn't require EU workers to register when they came to the UK, it has been difficult to measure the impact of ending free movement on the UK economy. But lower-paid sectors, including trucking and hospi-tality, have experienced labour shortfalls now they can no longer access labour from the EU. A joint study by the Centre for European Reform and the UK in a Changing Europe think tanks estimated that the shortfall in the UK labour market caused by Brexit was in the region of 330,000 workers in the year to June 2022. They estimated the hardest-hit parts of the economy included logistics (a shortfall of 128,000 workers or 8 per cent of the sector's workforce), hotels and restaurants (67,000 workers or 4 per cent of the workforce), retail (103,000 workers or 3 per cent of the workforce) and construction (46,000 workers or 2 per cent of the workforce).

Intuitively, you would expect the labour shortages to lead to higher wages, but data from the Migration Advisory Committee and the Office for National Statistics hasn't revealed a significant overall impact in wages in the UK economy as a result of ending free movement. And where there has been wage growth, like in lorry driving, it hasn't fixed the shortage problem. According to Logistics UK, the truckers' trade body, HGV driver wages rose 21 per cent in 2021 and another 7.3 per cent in the nine months to October 2022. And yet, at the same time, because of the rate at which the UK lorry driver population is retiring, the number of lorry drivers in employment remains stubbornly at 2019 levels when there was an estimated notional shortfall of 60,000 drivers. This is despite 'skills boot camps', and a 'Generation Logistics' publicity campaign to get younger people to sign up to a profession which is demographically very top-heavy.

In practice, the haulage industry has now started to adjust to life without a flexible supply of EU drivers, which often took up the slack over busy periods like the run-up to Christmas. Many UK companies, like Lincolnshire-based FreshLinc have started to train their own drivers, but there have been consequences from doing so, including rising costs. As Lee Juniper, FreshLinc's boss, put it: 'I'm not sure it's exactly a Brexit "success story". We've solved the problem, but we've had to pay through the nose for it.' That said, Juniper does recognise that the industry required investment and that the upside to Brexit is having a steadier pipeline of drivers and a reduction in use of agency drivers which has lowered damage rates to his fleet of trucks.

But in a sign of how tight the UK labour market has become, paying higher wages to drivers has caused a knock-on shortage of mechanics, many of whom held HGV licences so quit working in the garage to chase higher wages available on the road. 'The cost implications of huge pay increases have spilled over into maintenance engineers,' according to Paul Day, the managing director of Turners Soham, a Cambridgeshire trucking company with 2,500 lorries, who has also trained up many of his own drivers having previously relied heavily on drivers from the EU. 'It's forced up the wages of mechanics so transport costs have increased significantly in the last two years. That's been hurting the UK economy, but that's where we are.'

So for now, the trucking industry is back to working capacity as the slowdown in the UK economy in 2022 and 2023 has seen a sharp drop-off in demand. Although the unique factors that caused the 2021 drivers crisis – Covid-19, Brexit and UK tax policy reforms – is unlikely to repeat itself, the haulage industry knows that it is far from fixed. 'The industry is certainly not bulletproof. There's still a significant shortage of drivers in the UK,' says James Russell, the managing director of A.F. Blakemore & Son wholesale distributors, which has also invested heavily in training. 'If there was some sort of renewed pressure, less well-prepared parts of the industry could still come under strain pretty quickly.'

The industry's recruitment challenges pointed up the fact that even with new incentives and training, the UK labour market doesn't have a lot of spare capacity. During the Covid-19 pandemic it is estimated that around 500,000 people left the workforce, either retiring early or going off sick, and despite the government's best efforts, they haven't come back. And trucking, which requires drivers to work long hours and spend time away from home, is not a very attractive profession to many young people even at improved wage rates. The squeeze has caused frustration across other sectors, like hospitality and retail, to the point that even prominent Brexiters like Lord Wolfson, the head of the Next retail chain, have started to complain. As he said: 'In respect of immigration, it's definitely not the Brexit that I wanted.'

Ultimately both the quantity but also the composition of immigration into the UK is a political decision. Some UK industries that grew up as a result of free movement – soft fruit growing, or rearing turkeys, say – will shrink or even disappear altogether if the government is not able to give producers sufficient access to labour to make their industries work. In 2021, as a result of free movement ending, the UK reared about a million fewer turkeys than before Brexit and come Christmastime made up the shortfall by importing birds, mainly from Poland. Crudely speaking, the UK can either allow Polish workers into the UK to help rear and process turkeys, or ban Polish workers and import the birds from Poland.

That is scant consolation to lower-wage industries where employees are not paid enough to qualify for skilled visas and are left clamouring for more occupations to be included on the 'Shortage Occupations List' in order to fully operate, let alone grow, their businesses. A survey by the British Chambers of Commerce published in January 2023 found that over 80 per cent of UK small and medium-sized businesses reported facing challenges recruiting enough staff – with hospitality and manufacturing firms most likely to report difficulties. 'With an anaemic economy and low productivity, the Government must take immediate steps to ease the considerable labour pressures on businesses – we can't afford to wait any longer,' the chamber said.

Post-Brexit governments have so far been unmoved by such pleas from business interests, arguing that only by sticking to their guns on immigration policy will industry be incentivised to invest in training, improve productivity and raise wages. They also point out that the UK's skilled worker salary threshold of £26,200 is generous by European standards and covers more than 60 per cent of occupations in the UK. In France and Germany the skilled worker visa kicks in at €50,000 a year but of course those countries, being part of the EU single market, have access to a flexible pool of cheaper labour that can ebb and flow with demand.

Farming

The UK's new points-based system, while actually exceeding the vast majority of pre-Brexit predictions in terms of numbers of visas issued, still doesn't provide that same flexibility. That can create real challenges in jobs like tourism, agriculture or hospitality that rely on seasonal flows of labour. The government has introduced some seasonal worker programmes for agricultural and other workers which are due to taper away over time to incentivise the use of local labour, but the farming industry in particular has warned that the numbers are just not sufficient.

The National Farmers Union says that labour shortages peaked at 40 per cent of need in 2022, and averaged 15 per cent over the course of the year, with the horticulture sector worst affected. Fruit and vegetables, plants and flowers are going unpicked, the NFU said in a November 2022 letter to the immigration minister, which will lead to 'significant financial loss for British producers and nutritious food being wasted'. This is an example of where labour shortages have translated into lower output, not higher wages or better jobs for local people.

Education

Shifting the composition of UK migration away from favouring the EU also has a knock-on effect for the UK's position in its own neighbourhood. Take education, where during membership EU students could pay 'home' fees at UK universities and take part in the EU's educational exchange schemes, like the Erasmus, which the UK has now quit. In the first year after Brexit the number of EU students enrolling in British universities has more than halved, but the EU numbers were replaced by an increase in students from China, India and Nigeria. This superficially fits with the 'global Britain' vision, but these students are not a like-for-like replacement for the EU students from France, Germany and Italy. EU students studied a more diverse range of subjects than their Chinese or Indian counterparts who tend more towards courses in business management, engineering and computer science. For UK universities looking to forge and maintain research links with universities in Europe the post-Brexit immigration system makes it harder to maintain that pipeline. For a European student looking to study overseas, the UK is now just another possible choice, alongside the US, Australia or Singapore.

NHS

Health is another area where a sharp decline in EU doctors, nurses and dentists coming to work in the UK after Brexit has seen the slack being taken up by medical professionals from the rest of the world. But as with the education sector, the flows from the rest of the world are not a like-for-like replacement for EU health workers. For example, the NHS has struggled to recruit enough anaesthetists and cardio-thoracic surgeons from outside the EU since Brexit. In nursing, even though rest-of-world recruitment rose from 800 to 18,000 a year in the decade to 2022, that is still insufficient to make up for ongoing short-ages. Dentistry is another immigration pinch-point. The rate of EU and EFTA dentists registering to practise in the UK has halved since the EU referendum, but unlike for doctors and nurses, there has been no increase in non-EU dentists to compensate. The result is that Germany and Italy, for example, have about 70 per cent more dentists per head of population than the UK. The English reputation for bad teeth looks unlikely to improve any time soon. More seriously, bad teeth are linked to bad health outcomes which means more strain on the NHS. In summary, according to the Nuffield Trust, the health affairs think tank, for the NHS overall, 'Brexit has been another blow to resilience already stretched to breaking point'.

Social care and GPs

When key professions are added to the Shortage Occupations List (SOL) to make it easier to bring in overseas staff, it doesn't always solve the problem. The UK has a massive shortage of social care workers, with 165,000 full-time equivalent vacancies in 2022. For that reason, care workers have been put on the SOL but the lower salary requirement is still too high because care workers outside London, south-east England and Scotland aren't paid enough to meet even the reduced pay threshold to get a visa. As a result, the desperate shortage goes unaddressed. As the UK and a Changing Europe think tank observed in its 2023 report on post-Brexit immigration, perversely for a government that has promised to 'level up' the UK's regions, this 'inherent bias' towards the higher-paying London and South East makes it even harder for those in the UK's poorer areas to recruit migrant workers.

It is also ironic that while post-Brexit governments have often suggested that business could fix labour shortages by paying British workers better, they have failed to do just that in the one shortage occupation – care work – where the government could make a difference. The independent Migration Advisory

Committee that advises the government on immigration matters recommended the government set rates of at least £1 above statutory minimum wage in the public sector to attract more care workers into the profession, but the government has failed to act on the suggestion in England, unlike the devolved administrations in Scotland and Wales. It appears the government would prefer to rely on immigration to fix social care worker shortages, rather than raising taxes and increasing investment.

Even when the points-based system functions smoothly – and judged on its own terms the UK system has worked pretty efficiently since Brexit – it still creates pain and cost for business. European businesses that before Brexit could shift employees seamlessly into the UK now have to spend several weeks and thousands of pounds to bring staff into the UK. For an employee with a family, costs could run up to £20,000 for a five-year term. A one-size-fits-all visa system is also disproportionately painful for smaller and medium-sized enterprises. Previously, these smaller operations were able to access EU labour visa-free so never had to deal with the cost and bureaucratic headaches of obtaining visas out of the UK Home Office. Medium-skilled jobs that cross the salary threshold – a Polish bricklayer, or a French patisserie chef – now require often quite small businesses to battle visa bureaucracy in a way they didn't before Brexit. This can in practice limit the inflow of talent to the UK, particularly in service industries. An acute example of this can be seen in GP practices, which are in effect run as small businesses independent from the NHS. General practice medicine is increasingly reliant on overseas workers with 48 per cent of all trainee GPs in 2022 requiring visas, according to the British Medical Association. The problem is that only a shade over 10 per cent of GP practices had paid up to £1,500 to register with the Home Office to become a sponsor for skilled worker visa applicants by late 2022. The result is that international trainees looking to stay and work in the UK after they qualify have a very small pool of employers to choose from, so many don't stay in the UK, despite training here. That, as the Royal College of GPs told the government, is 'nonsensical' for a country where GP numbers have flatlined since 2015.

Ultimately, much of the sentiment that drove the UK to end free movement is reflected in the tribal nature of British politics.

Leavers have consistently held tougher views on immigration than Remainers, but surveys of British public opinion show that attitudes have started to shift since Brexit. In 2016 more than 80 per cent of Leave voters said they wanted to see immigration reduced, according to pollster Ipsos MORI, but by 2022 that figure had shrunk to 64 per cent – that's still two-thirds of Leavers, but it points to a direction of travel. For Remainers, the proportion wanting to reduce immigration fell from 43 per cent in 2016 to just 23 per cent in 2022 – less than a quarter. That's not the same as saying there is public support for returning to free movement, but it does suggest that public attitudes towards a fairly open immigration policy may be shifting as labour shortages and price rises continue to bite. Or as Professor Jonathan Portes of King's College London and Madeleine Sumption of the Oxford Migration Observatory observed in their report on future immigration policy for the UK in a Changing Europe, there are signs that for future governments – while the tensions between the political demands to curb migration and the economic demand for a more liberal approach have not disappeared – they may be 'less of a constraint' in the future.

7

Wish You Were Here

During his speech setting out a vision for post-Brexit Britain in Greenwich in February 2020 Boris Johnson, as well as lionising the UK's imminent rebirth as a global trading power, also recalled that the UK's relations with 'our closest neighbours' in the EU extended far beyond trade. The prime minister, who attended the European School in Brussels between the ages of eight and eleven, said he fully understood the need for continued cultural and scientific exchange between Europe and the UK after Brexit. 'In all these other areas, I see the same need for warmth,' Johnson said, promising that he would preserve 'cooperation for friendship and exchange, and *va et vient*' – coming and going – 'for academics, students and businesses, but', he added ominously, 'I see no need to bind ourselves to an agreement with the EU.'

As ever, Johnson delivered his lines with brio, but the last part of that sentence was shot through with a breezy cakeism that would end up carelessly destroying much of what he professed to want to protect. A great deal of the *va et vient* of daily life between the UK and the EU depends on agreements. First and foremost, of course, the free movement of people itself. But there are also schemes like group passports for school trips, or the EU's other official exchange programmes, like Erasmus+ for students or the Horizon Europe programme for scientific research. Those two schemes alone pool €120 billion to facilitate networks of education and research across the continent. But as the trade deal negotiations came to a close in 2020, Johnson decided at the last minute not to join Erasmus+. And while the UK did negotiate to retain associate membership of Horizon Europe, its participation in the scheme was blocked by the European Commission for the first three years because the Johnson government was failing to implement the deal it had agreed for post-Brexit trading arrangements in Northern Ireland.

But even outside these formal schemes, the ending of free movement and the imposition of border checks and controls has thrown sand into the gears of a wide range of EU–UK human interactions. In the creative industries, for example, TV production crews and touring musicians now need expensive documents to travel with their cameras and instruments along-side multiple flavours of work visa to play gigs in the EU. Schools across Europe that used to come on trips to the UK every year are now no longer able to use ID cards or group passports to bring their children to the UK, so many have stopped. The lack of a Youth Mobility Scheme for 18–30-year-olds (of the kind the UK enjoys with much more distant countries like Australia, Canada, and Japan) also stops thousands of young Brits and Europeans earning their way across each other's countries, working as au pairs, for example, or as *seasonaires* doing a summer in a Spanish campsite or a winter in a French ski resort. All of these activities have become substantially more expensive and complex as a result of Brexit.

The UK government believes that it is a virtue of 'global Britain's' points-based immigration system that it treats all countries of the world equally. But it makes little sense to treat the EU in the same way as the rest of the world for one very simple reason: the EU is an awful lot closer. It's a statement of the obvious, but the UK is physically connected to Europe by a tunnel; the continent can be reached by low-cost flights and cheap cross-Channel ferries that can cost less than a train ticket from London to Manchester. So while global stars like Ed Sheeran or Elton John might have the financial and artistic muscle to embark on a world tour, for most British musicians, international touring is more likely to consist of a chance to play in a music festival in Paris, Vienna or Berlin, or do maternity cover for the second violin of a city orchestra in Barcelona or Bonn. After Brexit, the added paperwork now means that for many it is no longer worth the hassle or the cost.

The costs of Brexit are counted in terms of lost GDP and trade, but often overlooked is the less quantifiable, human cost that comes from building back borders between the UK and our closest neighbours – the friendships never formed, the businesses never started, the artistic and scientific collaborations that never got off the ground. An April 2023 survey by the travel industry body ABTA found that the number of British citizens working in the EU travel industry in frontline roles such as travel reps, ski guides or chalet hosts fell by more than two-thirds since Brexit. That equates to tens of thousands of mostly young Brits missing out on formative experiences that previous generations enjoyed, many going on to start careers and found businesses in the travel sector.

Culture is also a huge British export worth around £30 billion a year; half of that income is from the EU. Post-Brexit restrictions on travel to the EU threw up barriers to all kinds of workers in the sector. It was not just the new visa-free limit of being able only to spend a maximum of 90 days in the EU during any 180-day period, but as with all so-called 'fly-in, fly-out' services, many activities – like performing in a band, say – now required permits and visas. To make matters trickier for small performers, permits and visas differ from EU country to EU country. For a big company with legal advisers and a compliance department, such obstacles are manageable, even if they do add to costs, but for a freelance cameraman, an exhibition curator or a young fashion model starting their trade, those costs and bureaucratic headaches quickly become prohibitive. One typical story was that of Netty Miles, a freelance events producer who was trying to deliver a touring science exhibition to Brussels in early 2022 but was told she needed a 'Professional Card' to operate in Brussels. This would have required a £250 medical exam, a £100 criminal records check and an interview at the Belgian embassy – all of which could take up to eight weeks. The job was on the cusp of being cancelled when someone found a loophole in Belgian law that meant that, because the science exhibition also contained the work of an artist, Miles and her crew could use a temporary exemption that allows 'artists and their assistants' to work permit-free.

This is just one quickly forgotten, nondescript case among thousands of such interactions, but it is not hard to see how such frictions deter not only UK workers from seeking work in the EU, but also EU cultural organisations, which are themselves often strapped for cash and short of time, going through the headache of hiring British acts and talent when hassle-free alter-native are available from inside the EU. And of course it is those starting out in their careers who are worst affected. A performance permit costing a few hundred euros is nothing to a big name performer who can afford administrative assistance, but can be the difference between a tour being viable or non-viable for a lesser-known artist touring venues in the Netherlands or Germany.

The Bands That Are Not Playing On

Among the worst-affected groups have been musicians. They not only need permits to perform like other artists, but also special documents – 'ATA Carnets' – to temporarily transport their equipment over the Channel and prove it is not for sale or export. Touring bands also fall foul of 'cabotage' rules for truck drivers which limit the number of stop-offs UK lorries can complete as they drive around the EU – which obviously doesn't work for a gigging band stopping in a new city every few nights. A survey by the House of Commons petitions committee found that 80 per cent of musicians that replied said that the new rules and bureau-cracy were likely to deter them from touring in Europe. Musicians with antique classical instruments made from rare woods that are now protected under the CITES convention on endangered species require additional permits in order to travel with their instruments. To make matters more complicated they can only enter the EU at ports that are designated for CITES permits and, bizarrely, the Eurostar terminal is not one of those ports. All of this bureaucracy can add many hundreds of euros of cost to a trip, which is often too much for a touring musician who survives on a share of the gate receipts at any gig and the chance to sell some merchandise – which of course needs another declaration in order to be shipped to the EU.

Not surprisingly, the impact of all this red tape has weighed heavily on a British industry that UK Music, the trade body, estimates is worth £5.8 billion a year and supports 200,000 jobs, generating £2.9 billion in exports – a significant chunk of which income comes from the EU. It is difficult to quantify the costs of Brexit for the music industry in simple financial terms, but in many ways the deeper cost is to the UK's soft power and cultural reach. A survey of the rosters of music festivals in Spain,

Hungary and Germany by Best for Britain, which campaigns for 'closer relationships with Europe and the world', found that the number of British musicians booked to perform at the festivals had fallen by 45 per cent in 2022 compared to the pre-Brexit period of 2017–19. Even established acts and theatre companies have struggled. The National Theatre cancelled a touring production of *The Curious Incident of the Dog in the Night-Time* in 2021, with managers saying that additional costs for visas and the lack of clarity around social security contributions had made the tour financially unviable. They had still not returned to Europe to tour by mid-2023. 'Luvvies' labours lost' was how the *Daily Mail* put it.

Unfortunately, despite huge amounts of lobbying, a solution to the problems facing touring musicians has not been found. More than 100 of the UK's biggest stars from classical and pop music – from Simon Rattle to Elton John – wrote to *The Times* soon after the Brexit deal came into force in early 2021 to warn that the new rules would leave many acts unviable. 'The deal done with the EU has a gaping hole where the promised free movement for musicians should be.' Since then, in some countries, like Spain, the cost of touring permits has been reduced, but musicians are still finding themselves having to navigate a patchwork of bureaucracies in order to go and perform. In December 2022, nearly two years after the Brexit deal was signed, Deborah Annetts, the chief executive of the Independent Society of Musicians, told MPs that Brexit was still 'an unmitigated disaster' for the music industry. 'Before Brexit, before we had the TCA, musicians could travel freely backwards and forwards to the EU. We had – and I hope will have again – a thriving creative industries sector, post-Brexit; musicians are telling us that it is simply economically not viable to tour into the EU any more. The figures do not work. They have almost given up, I would say.'

Travel Industry: No Passport, No Job

Musicians are only one category of workers that have found their old pathways to the Continent blocked by Brexit. Another is the outbound travel worker, usually a young person in their 20s or early 30s, who took up seasonal work in the EU helping to staff campsites, bars and skiing chalets for UK companies servicing British tourists in Europe. For many, such jobs were an entry-point into an industry worth over £15 billion a year in the EU alone. The Association of British Travel Agents (ABTA) says that a total of around 15,000-20,000 mostly young people a year were working in the EU before Brexit, with the majority taking advantage of what was called the 'posted workers directive', that enabled UK workers on UK contracts to work in the EU. But the ending of free movement has made it massively more difficult for UK companies to send UK staff into Europe. The obvious difficulty is that UK nationals can only spend three months (90 days) in the EU at a stretch, when the travel season (winter or summer) typically lasts for six months. That restriction is also not workable for a coach driver who typically would have spent 200 days a year in Europe before Brexit. And in every country except for Ireland, UK workers now need permits and visas, with EU countries having differing regimes, often designed to protect local workers from outside competition. UK tour-guiding qualifications, for example, aren't easily recognised in France or Malta, providing another block on UK workers.

The process for getting a work permit and visa for the French Alps gives a flavour of the new barriers that Brexit has thrown up. Jimmy Torre, the general manager of European Pubs, which operates restaurants and bars across the French Alps, estimates that the five-stage process of obtaining a permit costs his company around €500 per UK staff member, not including staff time used to process the applications. The whole process can take three months to complete and requires newly arrived bar staff to take two or three trips down the mountain, including chest X-rays for TB and €250 of other medical tests before they can obtain a multi-annual visa – *la carte de séjour pluriannuelle* – which enables them to work for six months a year for three years. That's great, but of less help than it sounds for an industry where there is an 80 per cent annual staff turnover. Not surprisingly, the impacts of these new bureaucratic hurdles have been huge. Charles Owen of Seasonal Businesses in Travel (SBiT), a UK trade group for British travel companies operating in the EU, said that even with intensive lobbying of the French government to try to speed up the process, the number of UK workers in the Alps has more than halved, from 9,000 before Brexit to around 2,500 in the

2022–3 season. The picture is even worse in Austria, Sweden, Germany, Spain and Italy, according to Owen.

It would be tempting to dismiss the plight of ski bums galli-vanting around the Alps, but the reality is that such jobs offered opportunity to the less privileged. Rich kids can happily pay their own way; it's the less well-off who need to work their passage. For many of today's tourism industry leaders, their own start in the business was through guiding and repping in the EU. People like Andrew Burden, the operations director for Venue Holidays, a small UK business that sells 7,000 campsite holidays a year in France, Italy and Spain. His own path into the travel industry began with working summer seasons on EU campsites, but now he sees those opportunities shrinking before his eyes for the next generation. Before Brexit, Burden had employed 50 mostly young British seasonal workers on his campsites; now he has only three experienced UK managers for whom it's worth going through the bureaucratic hoops. For young British people, the cost is not worth it.

'It's incredibly sad. This situation is actually worse than in pre-Maastricht days,' says Burden. 'Basically we don't recruit from the UK any more. The first question my recruiting team now have to ask is, "Have you got EU residency?" and if they say, "No," we can't take this application further.' As ABTA's public affairs director Luke Petherbridge observed when giving evidence in Parliament, Brexit has narrowed the path by which young people could go and learn languages and experience culture and life in European countries. 'We have blocked the ability for young UK nationals to do that at the moment. It seems deeply regrettable that we have done that,' he told the House of Lords European Affairs Committee, urging the govern-ment to strike a youth mobility deal with the EU. 'The UK government should look at that, particularly as we include it in trade deals all over the place at the moment. It seems illogical that we will not look at it with our nearest economic partners.'

Indeed. The failure to build routes for young Europeans and Brits to live and work in each other's countries is one of the silent tragedies of Brexit, where young people have been caught in the crossfire between ideological UK positions on immigra-tion and the strict European defence of the EU single market. The determination in Brussels that the UK, having quit the bloc, should not be able to 'cherry-pick' any aspect of EU membership has cut both ways, despite the economic benefits of cooperation that accrue to both sides. Young Italians or Spaniards who want to come and work in a UK bar or restaurant for six months to brush up on their English are now blocked from doing so, just like young Brits going in the other direction. Those kinds of jobs don't pay enough to qualify for the UK's £26,200 skilled worker visa.

And money doesn't always talk in this context. UK tourism is worth €7.5 billion a year to the French economy and supports 37,000 jobs in France directly and about 100,000 jobs on top of that, according to ABTA, but that doesn't mean France can suddenly grant exceptions to UK workers that it doesn't grant to other non-EU countries. French politicians, like British ones, have to deal with local interests, where tour guides or ski instructors have no interest in letting British competitors steal their lunches. It is a bitter irony that it was only in May 2020 that UK-qualified ski and snowboard instructors won a seven-year legal battle in the French courts for the right to teach in the Alps – a win for free and fair competition that was enforced by the very European Court of Justice so reviled by Brexiters, and a win now rendered sadly moot by Brexit.

Au Pairs and School Trips

Brexit has also put up barriers to young Europeans and school-children who want to come to the UK. As with young Brits, it is the least well-off who are most disadvantaged. The au pairs system, which provided cultural exchange and affordable live-in childcare to around 45,000 British families before 2020, is another casualty. At its best, the system facilitated cultural exchange while enabling middle-class families to juggle their careers, with doctors, nurses and police providing typical host families for au pairs according to the British Au Pair Agencies Association (BAPAA). For Mark Lilley, an oil trader from Chingford, east London, who is a single parent and had an au pair to help care for his 11-year-old daughter, Paige, the system worked perfectly, until Brexit. His final au pair, from Spain, was doing a master's, so while Paige was at school she was free to study. 'She improved her English and got to spend time in the UK, she gave Paige Spanish classes and helped with child-care – everyone was happy, it was win–win,' Lilley told me in 2021. Not any more. Before Brexit, more than 90 per cent of au pairs came from the EU and European Economic Area (EEA) countries, but that route has now dried up entirely since au pairs are not on the SOL and do not qualify for a skilled worker visa. This was a deliberate choice of the Johnson government. When the industry lobbied to provide an affordable path for au pairs, perhaps by reinstating the Au Pair Visa that was scrapped in 2008 after being made redundant by EU free movement rules, the government refused. As Kevin Foster, the then immigration minister in Johnson's government, wrote in a letter to BAPAA in early 2021, 'the UK's points-based immigration system will not offer a dedicated route for au pairs'.

Similarly, European schoolchildren have found themselves casualties of Brexit purism after the British government took the decision to remove the right of EU nationals to use their national ID cards to enter the UK. At the same time, the Johnson government shut down the so-called 'List of Travellers' group passport system that enabled entire classes of EU schoolchildren to enter the UK together on school trips. That was a blow for many EU schools that had children who either only had an ID card – so needed to spend money to get a passport – or did not have an EU passport at all. Most EU schools have a rule that 'all go, or none go', so for schools with children that were, say, refugees from Afghanistan or Syria, that meant obtaining visas. This is expensive, and in some circumstances required in-person interviews, trips to Paris or a nearby regional capital. Not surprisingly many EU schools voted with their feet.

For many teachers, like Isabelle Regiani who has taught English for over 20 years, the new rules ended a long-standing tradition of taking children to the UK. In 2021 the best she could do for her class at the Jean Jaurès middle school in the Franco-German border town of Sarreguemines was to take them to Calais, which at least had been ruled by the monarchs of England for more than 200 years from 1347 to 1558. As she put it: 'We'll have a walk on the beach in Calais and we'll see the cliffs, and I'll say, "See, there's the white cliffs of Dover."' Unless the class visa system is reinstated, Regiani says she has given up any hope of taking another trip to England, and Ireland is too expensive and doesn't have the same network of host families as the UK which helped to keep trips affordable. 'After the war in Ukraine my school has welcomed 15 Ukrainian teenagers. If they were to go on a trip to England, they not only would need a passport, but also a visa that would cost them around €100 and that they would have to go and pick up at the embassy in Paris. Imagine the costs!' she says.

Some schools did try, but reported 'Kafkaesque' brushes with the UK immigration system that rejected visa applications for kids on prepaid, group school trips for reasons that no one could fully understand. Take the case of a class of 12- and 13-year-olds from Collège les Hauts Grillets middle school in Saint-Germain-en-Laye, an hour's drive west of Paris, who had hoped to visit Stratford-upon-Avon in March 2023. The trip to William Shakespeare's birthplace was meant to be the perfect introduction to English literature and culture, but instead three of the children who did not hold EU passports (their parents were from Nigeria, China and Georgia but had regularised visas status in France) were refused visas despite being on an organised €450 trip, supervised by teachers and staying with a host family in Stratford. A fourth student, from Cambodia, who made an identical application, was given a visa for reasons the school does not understand.

The visa applications cost €120 and the interviews left the families feeling profoundly unwanted. Two of the Home Office rejection letters said the children had failed to prove they had 'parental consent' for the trip, despite travelling to visa interviews with their parents and signing an online parental consent form with the school. Edward Hisbergues, the boss of the company that organised the four-day outing, the exquisitely named PG Trips, said the company had sent 15,000 children a year to the UK over a 40-year period and, in all that time, not left a single one behind. And yet the Home Office was not satisfied these children were not a flight risk. As Hisbergues said, it was 'truly ridiculous'. Fadila Mérioua, the English teacher in the school's international section, was left in despair. 'I have been a teacher for 26 years, and never seen anything like this. It was really like something out of a Kafka novel,' she said. The school's head said there would be no more school trips until visa conditions improved. Such experiences are not isolated according to the school trip industry, and the negative signal they send is resonating through school networks, causing silent but profound damage to the UK's reputation abroad.

The hurdles for school trips cut both ways. Before Brexit, according to the British Educational Travel Association, 1.2 million EU students under the age of 18 visited the UK each year to attend English language schools, for school trips, or take part in cultural and sporting events. That meant revenue for hostels and language schools, but also as a source of income for local families who hosted the students. But the human loss far exceeds the financial one. As Jenny Collings, a host in Chester with two grown-up daughters studying modern languages reflected when the visitors started to dry up in 2021, the children she had hosted over the years had encouraged her son to study French and German. 'It's exciting, it makes the world feel a bit bigger,' she said. 'It's given my son a real head start. He can often help with a word if a visitor is struggling. He's confident because of it and is used to mixing with the children.' As things stand, many thousands of children from the EU will be denied that experience every year, travelling instead to other countries where English is spoken, like Ireland and the Netherlands, if they can afford it, allowing the UK to slip further and further from its cultural moorings in Europe. Johnson promised to preserve the *va et vient* of EU–UK relationships, but that is not what he delivered.

8

Brexit and the Constitutional Conundrum

Two weeks before the June 2016 Brexit referendum John Major and Tony Blair went to Northern Ireland to make a joint appearance in the city of Derry/Londonderry. The two former prime ministers came with a shared message about the risks that Brexit would pose to political stability in the region and the constitutional integrity of the UK more generally. 'The very unity of the United Kingdom itself is on the ballot paper on June 23rd and a British exit from the European Union could tear apart the oldest union in world history,' Major told a hall filled with secondary school children. 'All the pieces of the peace process jigsaw would be thrown into the air and no one knows where those pieces would land.'

The students in the audience were too young to have any first-hand recollection of the three decades' of conflict in Northern Ireland that was ended by the 1998 Good Friday Agreement, the peace deal that was started on Major's watch but concluded under Blair. Earlier, the two former leaders had walked across the Peace Bridge that spans the River Foyle, connecting the city's mainly unionist Waterside enclave on the east bank with the largely nationalist Cityside on the west. They posed for pictures beneath the two cantilevered pylons that reach out from either side of the river, like hands from either community straining to touch but never quite able to meet in the middle.

The former PMs chose Derry/Londonderry because it was the city perhaps most closely connected in the British public imagination with the conflict that left over 3,700 people dead, including 13 unarmed Catholics in the infamous 'Bloody Sunday' incident of January 1972 when British paratroopers opened fire on an anti-internment protest in the city. But it wasn't just the the city's schoolkids for whom the Troubles were fading into the haze of recent history. Despite the fact that Brexit risked triggering the biggest constitutional upheaval for the UK since Ireland was partitioned in 1921, the issue of what leaving the EU would mean for the Union barely featured in the 2016 campaign.

The warnings of Major and Blair were dismissed as yet more 'Project Fear' by prominent members of the pro-Brexit Democratic Unionist Party (DUP) and leading British Brexiters. After more than a decade and a half of peace, Northern Ireland had disappeared from the front pages of British newspapers. This felt strange to me. Twenty years previously, as a young Fleet Street reporter, I'd written about little else: the closing down of the Maze prison where the IRA man Bobby Sands died on hunger strike; the annual Protestant–Catholic stand-off over the 12 July 'marching season' at Drumcree; the Docklands bombing of 1996; the horror of the 1998 Omagh bombing and – finally – the unexpected triumph of the Good Friday Agreement itself.

For good or ill, Northern Ireland had topped the national and international news agenda week in, week out. Every newspaper had a full-time correspondent in Belfast who understood the issues at stake. For me the day the Belfast/Good Friday Agreement became real was in November 1999 when I found myself right on deadline in Stormont Castle reporting to readers of the *Daily Telegraph* that Martin McGuinness had been handed the education portfolio in Northern Ireland's first power-sharing executive led by David Trimble. The former commander of the Derry IRA was now Minister for Education in a devolved Northern Ireland government, controlling a £1.6 billion budget and the education of every child in the North. The impossible had become possible. Like the ending of apartheid in South Africa, peace in Northern Ireland was something no one believed was possible until one day it finally happened.

And yet Fleet Street and the political class in Westminster had shed the institutional memory of what lay behind the Good Friday Agreement with amazing speed. Brexit didn't directly threaten the peace in Northern Ireland but, as Tony Blair observed to those schoolchildren, it unavoidably upset the delicate constitutional ambiguity that underpinned the

Good Friday Agreement. That 'carefully constructed foundation', as Blair called it, allowed the Nationalist community to live out an Irish existence, with an Irish-only passport, in exchange for giving up their armed struggle to oust the Brits. But for their part, Unionists had to accept the creation of north–south institutions of government as a tangible demonstration of the Irish identity in Northern Ireland. They also had to accept that if there was a reasonable prospect that a simple majority of Northern Ireland's electorate favoured Irish unification, then there would be a 'border poll' to confirm it.

In essence, the Good Friday Agreement resolved the conflicting aspirations of Unionists and Nationalists by allowing both sides to live in parallel constitutional realities. As Blair explained, Brexit would rock that compromise. 'If the United Kingdom votes to leave, it will create a unique situation here in Northern Ireland. The Republic of Ireland will be "in" and the UK "out". The border with the Republic of Ireland will then become the border of the European Union, with border controls, customs checks, both of which will be damaging to trade. That would be unforgivably irresponsible,' he said.

As it turned out, the voters of Northern Ireland opted to remain in the EU by a majority of 56 per cent to 44 per cent, but there were enough English Brexiters to ensure the UK as a whole voted to leave. And just as Major and Blair predicted, Brexit has indeed destabilised and polarised the politics of the North over the last seven years. Whole books have been written about the UK's post-Brexit negotiations over Northern Ireland and thousands of newspaper column inches expended on explaining 'backstops' and 'bullet points', 'protocols' and 'frameworks'. The details were sometimes obscure but beneath these complex constructs lay a stark choice between the prosecution of Brexit on the one hand, and the preservation of the Union on the other. Put another way, the harder you pushed Brexit, the more pressure you placed on the constitutional bonds of the Union – in Northern Ireland, but also in Scotland and Wales, as we shall see.

In Northern Ireland the constitutional conundrum of Brexit presented itself as an impossible 'trilemma': if a British government promised to leave the EU single market and customs union, then there would need to be a border – either 'north–south' in Ireland, or 'east–west' in the Irish Sea that separates Great Britain and Northern Ireland. The UK could not simultaneously promise to leave the EU single market and customs union without creating a border either in the Irish Sea or on the island of Ireland. The logic was inescapable: border checks had to be conducted somewhere – and since London, Brussels and Dublin all agreed a north–south trade border should never return in Ireland for the sake of peace – then logically that meant a border in the Irish Sea.

Over the last seven years different British prime ministers have responded very differently to this challenge. Theresa May was the first. Confronted by the logical reality of a customs border in the Irish Sea by the European Commission in early 2018, she recoiled. May told Parliament that such an arrangement would 'undermine the UK common market and threaten the constitutional integrity of the UK' and that '*no UK prime minister could ever agree to it*'. She took a long and tortuous road, but in the end she resolved the Brexit trilemma by agreeing that the UK would remain in a customs union with the EU while aligning with EU rules for goods trade 'unless and until' an alternative technological solution could be found to create an invisible north–south border on the island of Ireland.

This became known as the 'backstop', but since no such 'invisible' border existed anywhere in the world, no one believed this magical construct was likely to materialise any time soon. So May's deal effectively consigned the UK to membership of a customs union with the EU. Tory Brexiters deemed this unacceptable, since it meant the UK couldn't strike its own independent trade deals once Brexit had occurred, and Labour didn't come to May's rescue and lend their votes to put her deal over the line. The deal was therefore rejected by MPs, inexorably leading to May's political downfall in the summer of 2019 and opening the door of Downing Street to Boris Johnson.

Back in 2018 when May had dismissed the idea of an Irish Sea border at the Commons dispatch box as unthinkable, Johnson, then the foreign secretary, had been sitting on the front bench. As she spoke, he nodded along in agreement. But after coming to power on a promise to 'Get Brexit Done' that was precisely what Johnson signed up to – a border in the Irish Sea. The Protocol on Northern Ireland that Johnson agreed with Brussels in December 2019 essentially replaced May's 'backstop' with a 'frontstop'. He resolved the trilemma with a legally binding agreement to leave Northern Ireland in the EU's legal orbit for goods trade, VAT and subsidy policy. The deal avoided the return of a north–south trade border, but to achieve this left part of the UK under the direct jurisdiction of the European Court of Justice for trade purposes and created a trade border in the Irish Sea, complete with customs checks, regulatory compliance paperwork and physical border inspection posts.

This was the trade-off Johnson made to enable the rest of the UK – Great Britain – to make a clean break with Brussels. Leaked Whitehall risk assessments set out the costs of this Irish Sea trade border in great detail, but as Unionists cried betrayal, Johnson's tactic was simply to deny what he'd done. Interviewed on Sky television in December 2019 Johnson was asked directly if the Protocol would require checks on goods travelling from Great Britain to Northern Ireland. 'Will there be checks?' asked the presenter. 'No, absolutely not,' Johnson replied. The presenter gave him the opportunity to clarify, and Johnson again repeated the denial. 'There is no question of there being checks on goods going NI–GB or GB–NI,' he said. It was an untruth Johnson would assert repeatedly. In August 2020 as the exact terms of how that Irish Sea trade border were being thrashed out in talks in Brussels, Johnson was still in denial, telling ITV News: 'There will be no border down the Irish Sea – over my dead body.'

For all his obfuscations, Boris Johnson had simply made a different choice to Theresa May. And to be fair, leading figures in the Brexit movement had made no secret that a clean-break Brexit for Great Britain should be prioritised over political stability in Northern Ireland. In May 2018 as May's divorce negotiation was floundering in Brussels over the Northern Ireland question, Dominic Cummings, the former head of the Vote Leave campaign, published an open letter to Tory MPs warning them that Northern Ireland could not be allowed to stand in the way of Brexit. 'If you think that babble about "the complexity of the Irish border/the Union/peace" will get you all off the hook, you must be listening to the same people who ran the 2017 campaign,' he wrote. 'It won't. The public, when they tune back in at some point, will consider any argument based on Ireland as such obvious bullshit you must be lying.' The following summer, when Cummings went into Downing Street to serve as Johnson's de facto chief of staff, charged with pushing a Brexit deal over the line at any cost, he impressed the same point on the prime minister. As Cummings recalled in another blog written after leaving Number 10, he advised Johnson 'to do whatever it takes, [and] when officials start babbling about Ireland, the union, the rule of law and what not, we just keep bulldozing'.

Johnson did exactly as Cummings advised. And the Boris bulldozer was successful at delivering Brexit, even if it left a trail of constitutional debris in its wake. In one publicity stunt Johnson drove a 'Get Brexit Done' JCB digger, painted in Union flag colours, through a wall of plastic blocks emblazoned with the word 'gridlock', just to make the point. Cummings and Johnson calculated – correctly, given the 80-seat majority they secured at the December 2019 general election – that the majority of the British public didn't know or care much about Northern Ireland.

But Johnson's denials over the Irish Sea border created by the Northern Ireland Protocol didn't survive contact with reality. Unionists said they had been promised that Northern Ireland could participate fully in the UK Internal Market, but that was, and is, impossible to reconcile with the trilemma. When the Protocol came into force in January 2021 they quickly discovered that the Irish Sea border was very real. Traders in Great Britain encountered a mountain of paperwork to send goods to Northern Ireland and many stopped doing so. Residents of Northern Ireland also found their Amazon deliveries got delayed, and the famed garden centres of Ulster no longer stocked Scottish seed potatoes and had fewer English pot plants. Pets, including guide dogs, needed passports to go from Birmingham to Belfast and medicines licensed for use in the UK could no longer necessarily be distributed in Northern Ireland.

As the senior former Northern Ireland Executive Office official Andrew McCormick wrote, Johnson's false promises of 'unfettered access' could never be reconciled either with the Protocol itself, or with the subsequent agreements reached in

December 2020 on how the Protocol would actually be applied. But as McCormick also observed, Johnson's denials only succeeded in stoking the sense of betrayal among Unionists in Northern Ireland: 'The UK Government itself has clearly contributed to the sense of grievance strongly felt by many unionists over the Protocol,' he wrote.

This particular piece of Brexit history bears repeating because the difficulties in Northern Ireland arose directly from political choices made by successive post-Brexit governments in Westminster. They were not inevitable. Because the equation was simple: the harder the Brexit, the thicker the trade border in the Irish Sea, and the more tension that would create with the Unionist community. Indeed in June 2020, as it negotiated with Brussels over how the Irish Sea border would be implemented, the Johnson government made another explicit choice to prioritise a hard Brexit over the interests of Northern Ireland. The senior Unionist Edwin Poots, then Northern Ireland's agriculture minister, wrote to the Johnson government to warn that unless the UK brokered a Swiss-style veterinary agreement in which the UK would dynamically align with the EU, the Protocol would place 'unacceptable burdens' on Northern Ireland. 'We are always prepared to play a full role in making this work and it is my hope and expectation that UKG [UK government] will take a similar approach in working with us,' Poots wrote. His optimism was misplaced. Johnson ignored the request and went ahead and negotiated a trade deal without the veterinary or 'SPS' agreement that would have radically reduced checks on food and plant products at the Irish Sea border.

The UK's subsequent refusal to fully implement the deal soured relations between London and Brussels. This prolonged the fight over the implementation of the Irish Sea border, which in turn deepened the Unionist 'sense of grievance' that McCormick identified. The EU was also not blameless. The European Commission, egged on by member states, including France, that were piqued by Brexit, was far too slow to accept that the Irish Sea border created by the Protocol could not be enforced in anything like the same manner as the Dover–Calais border. The European Commission's hamfisted decision in January 2021, amid a vaccine shortage in the EU, to use the

Protocol's 'Article 16' emergency suspension clause to block the export of Covid-19 vaccines to Northern Ireland was a massive own goal. While the decision was almost instantly rescinded by Brussels it lit the blue touchpaper of Unionist opposition to the Protocol which is only just now beginning to be addressed.

At the very beginning of 2021 Arlene Foster, then the DUP Leader, had struck a bitter yet pragmatic tone on the Protocol, refusing to back calls from hardliners in her party to take unilateral action to block the deal. Interviewed on the *Andrew Marr Show* just days after the agreement came into force, Foster said that even though the DUP didn't vote for the Protocol it was now her job to 'mitigate against' issues caused by the deal. 'I could stand here and bemoan the fact that we've left the European Union with a protocol – I wish that wasn't the case – or I can now look for the opportunities as we move out of the EU,' she said. After Brussels briefly flirted with Article 16, Foster stopped backing calls for restraint. And the Johnson government, looking for a stick with which to beat the European Commission over the implementation of the Protocol, did nothing to tamp down the flames of Unionist opposition.

That first mistake was undoubtedly the EU's; it's also fair to say that during the three years of bitter recriminations that followed, Brussels also consistently opted not to rise to UK government provocations. The EU kept on negotiating in 2020 when the Johnson government tabled its first law-breaking legislation, the Internal Market Bill, that threatened to unilaterally rip up parts of the Protocol. It did the same again in 2022 after Boris Johnson tabled the even more sweeping Northern Ireland Protocol Bill that threatened to completely gut the deal. By then, Johnson had rowed in behind unionist arguments that the Protocol he had negotiated was a threat to Northern Ireland's place in the Union, and that the DUP's rejection of the Protocol was itself evidence of a breach with the 1998 Good Friday Agreement.

This approach helped to escalate concerns about the Protocol from practical issues about the movement of goods to a constitutional-level crisis. The European Commission, again, did not overreact. In fact in October 2021 the Commission had tabled a fresh set of 'easements' to reduce the operational impact of the Irish Sea border. Liz Truss, then foreign secretary, briefly

engaged with Brussels, inviting the EU's chief post-Brexit negotiator Maroš Šefčovič for a carefully choreographed stroll around
the frosty grounds of her Chevening country retreat in Kent in
January 2022. But by April 2022 it was clear that the promised
thaw in relations was not going to happen. EU–UK talks to fix
the agreement simply dried up. Again Westminster politics were
at play. During that spring, as Johnson's government was engulfed
in scandal, it had become apparent to Truss that the same hard-
line Brexiters who would brook no compromise with Brussels
could also be her political ticket to Downing Street. So she
ditched the talks and toughened the Northern Ireland Protocol
Bill at their request, deepening distrust and irritation in Brussels
yet further. Truss got to Downing Street but Northern Ireland's
politics slid deeper into the morass.

To his credit, Rishi Sunak took a different tack after coming
to power in autumn 2022. He quietly put Johnson and Truss's
Northern Ireland Protocol Bill on the backburner and, having
taken the legislative gun off the table, sent a team of officials
to Brussels to negotiate practical fixes to the Protocol. The
result was the Windsor Framework of February 2023 which,
while leaving Northern Ireland still following EU law for goods
trade, addressed many of the consumer-facing issues created by
the Protocol. The deal didn't remove the Irish Sea border, it
just sought to de-dramatise it. Pets no longer needed EU passports; individuals could send parcels across the Irish Sea without
customs forms; UK-registered medicines were available equally
in Northern Ireland, while English native oaks and Scottish
seed potatoes could once again be found in Ulster's garden
centres. The deal also obscured the practical plumbing of a
customs and regulatory border, forcing it back onto business
and away from consumers – an important consideration to
ensure that Unionists in Northern Ireland felt part of the UK
internal market. Announcing the deal, Sunak chose his words
carefully, saying that it removed 'any sense' of a border in the
Irish Sea – even if there were still some pipes carefully concealed
in the brickwork.

The Windsor Framework also tried to address the perceived
constitutional issues caused by leaving Northern Ireland under
the jurisdiction of a foreign court for some elements of trade.
Sunak couldn't magic away the legal reality of the Protocol –

where EU law applies in Northern Ireland the European Court of Justice will ultimately be the judge – but his deal did shrink the amount of EU law applying in the region. By getting the European Commission to agree that products made to UK food standards could circulate in Northern Ireland if they were labelled 'Not for EU' consumption, he ensured that a significant number of EU laws no longer needed to apply to all goods being consumed in the region.

The deal also took fresh steps to address the vital issue of 'consent'. Ever since the Protocol had come into force Unionists had complained, with justification, that the deal gave Northern Ireland no say over updates to laws being handed down from Brussels. They argued this left a yawning 'democratic deficit'. In 2020 the European Commission had agreed that every four years Northern Ireland's Assembly would hold a vote on whether to continue with the trade-related parts of the Protocol – a simple majority of the 90 legislators is required – but that still left Northern Ireland sucking up new rules whenever Brussels amended or expanded existing regulations. To address this issue the Windsor Framework added a so-called 'Stormont Brake' which, in exceptional circumstances, allowed Stormont to demand that the Westminster government challenge new EU laws, or amendments to existing applicable EU laws, that Northern Ireland felt it could not accept. It remains to be seen how this constitutional buffer will work in practice, but whatever its actual utility, the 'brake' was an important symbolic recognition that both the British government and the EU are sensitive to Northern Ireland's position post-Brexit – a sensitivity for much of the previous seven years that has been utterly lacking. While the hurdles in the way of using the Stormont Brake are significant, it does nonetheless carry the risk that Northern Ireland might diverge from single market rules sufficiently to put its ongoing participation in the single market at risk. So if the brake is ever pulled, the stakes will be high.

There can be no doubt that, just as Major and Blair predicted, Northern Ireland has been rocked by Brexit. In so far as Brexit is an expression of specifically English nationalism at the expense of the Union, it has also inevitably had a corollary effect on Irish nationalism in Northern Ireland. On the night of the 2016 referendum the late Martin McGuinness called for an immediate vote on Irish unity arguing that since the North had voted 56 per cent to remain in the EU that created a 'democratic imperative' for a border poll. It didn't. But Brexit inevitably puts a keener edge on questions of identity and allegiance that the Good Friday Agreement looked to push off into the distant future. A vote for unification is now also a vote to rejoin the EU. It is not surprising that, since Brexit, polling has revealed a clear polarisation of North Ireland's politics. Unionists are more likely to support Brexit and oppose the Protocol, while Nationalists are more likely to strongly oppose Brexit and support the Protocol. As Katy Hayward, a professor of political sociology and Brexit expert at Queen's University Belfast, put it, 'The Protocol has provided a small taster of what Irish unification would mean in the sense of practical as well as political division.'

And after three years of bitter in-fighting between London and Brussels, the political apparatus created by the Good Friday Agreement finds itself in need of even greater political life-support. A functioning executive is essential to deliver on the day-to-day needs of Northern Ireland's people. The Stormont Assembly has now been suspended for over a third of its lifetime. The system of cross-community vetoes, whereby both Unionist and Nationalist parties must agree to power-sharing, is also disenfranchising the 'non-aligned' voters that make up the growing centre-ground of the region's politics. As well as polarising Northern Ireland, internal Unionist divisions over the Protocol have also fractured the party's voting blocs enabling nation-alist Sinn Fein to become the largest party in the Stormont Assembly at the 2022 elections. The prospect of a Sinn Fein first minister has in turn further sharpened the debate about the long-term direction of Northern Ireland and stoked Unionist opposition to compromise. And for Nationalists arguing that unification is the road to a better future, over the last seven years Brexit also provided constant reminders that Northern Ireland is at the mercy of decision-making in a Westminster parliament that, to put it kindly, does not always take the region's best interests into account.

All of these forces feed into the political pressures now visible in Northern Ireland. As John Major said, there can be no knowing how the pieces of the jigsaw will fall, but they have been scattered by Brexit. For now, a vote for reunification still looks some way off. The rolling NI Life and Times (NILT) surveys – the benchmark annual survey of political and social attitudes in Northern Ireland – still shows support for the Union as the majority view. But support for a united Ireland has doubled since Brexit: from 14 per cent in 2015 to 30 per cent in 2021. Some other polls put the gap as even narrower, with majority support for unification among the younger generation. In another possible tell-tale for the future, census and survey data also show a fall in 'British-only' identity and a rise in 'Irish-only' identity, particularly among the 'Agreement generation'. It is this generation that will be most likely to be voting in a border poll.

All that is for the future. The immediate question is whether the Windsor Framework, after all the upheaval of the last seven years, can settle Northern Ireland back into a positive equilibrium, enjoying the benefits of simultaneous access to the UK and EU single markets. Certainly, after the confrontations of the Johnson years, more positive forces are now at play. As Sunak put it when selling his deal, 'Northern Ireland is in the unbelievably special position – unique position in the entire world, European continent – in having privileged access, not just to the UK home market, which is enormous . . . but also the European Union single market.' If Labour is elected in 2024 and goes on to complete the veterinary agreement that Edwin Poots originally asked for, that would further underpin the workability of a deal that is always going to grate on some Unionists. That year will also see Stormont vote for the first time on whether or not to remain in the full Protocol arrangements. If the Windsor Framework is bedding in, a 'yes' vote could provide another stepping stone to normalisation rather than a fresh focal point for division.

At the same time, the restoration of warmer diplomatic links between London and Dublin – which were plunged into the deep freeze for much of the Brexit process – will also be essential to making the Good Friday Agreement operate again, with the 'two governments working as co-guardians', in the words of the veteran Irish diplomat Tim O'Connor. Ultimately, after years of turbulence, Northern Ireland must be seen to benefit from the gradual retreat from Brexit puritanism on both sides of the Irish Sea. Everything must be done to capitalise on this new momentum, including drawing down promised high-profile investment from America to showcase the benefits of the deal. The landing of the Windsor Framework, despite objections from the likes of Boris Johnson and David Frost, has demonstrated that there is finally an emerging appetite for pragmatism in Brexit politics. The hope must be that that will spill over into other areas too.

Scotland and Wales

Northern Ireland has provided the clearest constitutional pinch-point caused by Brexit, but leaving the EU has also created fresh tensions with the devolved administrations in Scotland and Wales. Before Brexit, Brussels set the rules for the entire UK across a wide range of policy areas – from food standards to government subsidy policy – many of which were devolved. After exiting the EU those powers were transferred back to the UK. The challenge after Brexit was how to share out that power anew between the UK Parliament and the devolved administrations in Wales, Scotland and Northern Ireland (where the Protocol didn't keep Northern Ireland following EU law).

The resulting settlement has not been easy. Since 2016 both the Scottish and Welsh parliaments have frequently accused the government in Westminster of riding rough-shod over powers that were previously held in Edinburgh or Cardiff. These clashes often get little coverage in the English-centric British national media but are a lightning rod for nationalist sentiment and likely to be a continued source of friction in the future. After Brexit, but before the UK actually left the EU, the four governments of the UK worked together to establish what were called Common Frameworks to manage their differences in over 150 devolved policy areas that were impacted by leaving the EU. Many areas were uncontentious, but others, including environmental regulation, agriculture, food standards, animal welfare, transport and energy all had the capacity to inflame regional passions if policy that previously had been devolved to Edinburgh or Cardiff was now being handed down from on high in Westminster. Just as English nationalists hated 'taking dictation' from Brussels before Brexit, so Scottish and Welsh nationalists chafe against Westminster suddenly having renewed say over the way they run their countries.

On one level, post-Brexit intra-UK tensions are inevitable, given that Scotland's government is controlled by the Scottish National Party whose main political mission in life is to seek independence from the UK. But Brexit has provided fresh grist to the separatists' mill on an almost daily basis. The Common Frameworks policy was designed to create official forums to help resolve these tensions behind the scenes, but in practice the Westminster government has often opted to confront the devolved administrations in the name of 'Getting Brexit Done'. This has been a departure from the way the UK previously managed devolution. Before Brexit, differences between Westminster and the devolved governments were almost always resolved via the so-called 'Sewel Convention'. This is a legally non-binding understanding that says that the Westminster Parliament will 'not normally' legislate on devolved matters without the consent of the devolved legislatures. In practice, this convention incentivised both sides to keep negotiating in private to avoid a public constitutional clash. Westminster governments didn't want to be seen ramming through laws over the heads of governments in Edinburgh and Cardiff and so were incentivised to compromise before legislation crossed the line. This in turn provided leverage to the Scottish and Welsh governments. And until 2016 the Sewel Convention worked well, with legislative consent being denied only nine times out of the 350 occasions on which it was sought, according to the Institute for Government.

After Brexit, it's been a different matter. Scotland didn't vote for Brexit (62 per cent of Scots voted to remain) and so the Scottish Parliament withheld consent for the 2018 EU Withdrawal Act. Not surprisingly, the Westminster government pushed ahead arguing that this was an 'abnormal' circumstance in which the Sewel Convention had to be ignored in order to give effect to an international treaty agreed by the British government. But since then Westminster has passed five more pieces of hugely significant legislation to lay the legal foundations of post-Brexit Britain all without Scottish consent. The Welsh Senedd has also refused consent for several key pieces of post-Brexit law. The most fundamental of these was the Internal Market Bill 2020 which built the framework for the UK's post-Brexit economy. As well as requiring Scotland and Wales to accept common standards with England on food and environmental issues, it also handed the Westminster government sweeping financial powers to spend money in Scotland and Wales in ways that would cut across devolved areas, from education programmes to road building and green grants to deliver the net zero revolution.

The Scottish and Welsh governments were both enraged, accusing the government in Westminster of a 'power grab'. Nicola Sturgeon, the then Scottish First Minister, called the Bill 'an abomination' while the Welsh government – which unlike the SNP government is avowedly a pro-Union government – called it an 'an attack on democracy and an affront to the people of Wales'. Tensions haven't eased since then, not helped by leading Conservatives taking an increasingly confrontational approach to devolution during the Johnson and Truss premierships. When campaigning for Downing Street in the summer of 2022, Truss dismissed Sturgeon as an 'attention-seeker', adding that the 'best thing to do with Nicola Sturgeon is ignore her'. David Frost went further, arguing in a newspaper column for the *Daily Telegraph* that the Scottish National Party needed to be confronted. 'In the current institutional set-up, a constructive relationship is a sign of failure,' he wrote. 'Instead, we need disagreement, vigorous argument, and consistent political challenge to the SNP world-view.'

That has certainly been the outcome of Brexit. Hardly a day passes when the Scottish National Party does not issue a press release arguing that Brexit has been foisted on the Scottish people to the detriment of their nation. Whether it's tomato shortages on supermarket shelves, the collapse in the numbers of EU students coming to Scottish universities or labour shortages for rural industries, the SNP never misses a chance to argue for independence and the opportunity to rejoin the EU that it would bring. To take but one example, in the summer of 2022 the Scottish government proposed a 'rural visa' scheme to attract workers to remote areas of Scotland, which was overruled by the UK government. 'Scotland deserves better,' thundered the SNP. 'We did not vote for Brexit or the Tory government yet both are causing huge damage to rural industries, making it crystal clear the only way to protect Scotland's world-class industries is to become an independent Scotland with a seat at the table of the European Union.' In a similar vein, Scotland's government also refused consent for the UK's post-Brexit subsidy framework which replaced the EU State Aid regime. SNP ministers argued the new system 'completely overrides the devolution settlement' by giving UK ministers powers to spend directly in devolved areas 'without the oversight and consent of the Scottish Parliament and Scottish ministers'.

The Welsh government has also kicked back against Westminster for its plans to use powers in the Internal Market Act to fund projects – for example adult literacy and numeracy programmes – that it says clearly cut across devolved areas of government. The distribution of centrally administered funds, like the Community Renewal Fund in 2020 or more recently the UK Shared Prosperity Fund have infuriated the Welsh government. Vaughan Gething, the Welsh economy minister, said the UK government approach was designed to systematically exclude the Welsh government and amounts to 'a new era of aggressive centralisation'. He added: 'As power grabs go, this one is about as subtle as an earthquake.' Inevitably more confrontation lies ahead unless the Westminster government seeks to work constructively with Wales and Scotland. The Welsh government is testing the new limits to its powers with legislation on single-use plastics and a decision to halt all new road-building projects, including a relief road for the M4 motorway that was once championed by Boris Johnson. The Scottish government took an equally strong stance in opposing this aspect of the Act, but the Northern Ireland Executive was divided as the DUP were less unhappy about the UK government spending money in Northern Ireland.

In short, with powers coming back from Brussels, Brexit perhaps inevitably creates a degree of friction with the devolved administrations, but the management of those tensions is also a matter of choice. The fact that the Welsh government, which doesn't harbour separatist ambitions, has clashed so hard with Westminster speaks to the constitutional side-effects of English Conservatives using Brexit powers to actively roll back more than 20 years of Scottish and Welsh devolution. Rishi Sunak, unlike Truss and Johnson, has signalled a superficially more consensual approach, but post-Brexit legislation has already shifted the balance of power. The informal Sewel Convention worked because both sides respected it, with cooperation rather than confrontation the preferred outcome. Given the number of times that the devolved governments have withheld consent for legislation since Brexit, it is not clear whether that particular constitutional genie can now be put back in its bottle. But in a world where the UK urgently needs to demonstrate to the outside world that it is capable of finding a new, post-Brexit equilibrium, the spectacle of a constantly 'disunited' kingdom surely doesn't help.

Part II

What to Do About It

9

Ending the Politics of Betrayal

The headline on the report in the *Guardian* was nothing, if not arresting: 'Revealed: secret cross-party summit held to confront failings of Brexit'. The newspaper reported in breathless terms that a group of politicians, business chiefs, former Whitehall officials (and a couple of journalists, myself included) had been gathered together by the Ditchley Foundation in Oxfordshire for a pow-wow on Brexit. The discussion took place at Ditchley Park, a magnificent Grade I listed Palladian stately pile that once appeared in an episode of *Downton Abbey*, and is like a step back in time. The house, with its tapestries, oil paintings and grand marble fireplaces, served as a country retreat for Churchill in the early years of the Second World War when it was feared that Chequers was too obvious a target for German bombers. Today, it is home to the Ditchley Foundation, which was set up in 1958 to foster better understanding in international relations. The Foundation hosts residential conferences which collect people from all corners of public life and, for a couple of days, sequesters them away to discuss the priority issues of the day. On the Ditchley agenda that first week in February 2023 was a private discussion about how Brexit might be made to work better.

The meeting was private, but not secret. Given all the toxicity that pervaded the Brexit debate nearly seven years after the 2016 referendum, the intention was to try to create a bipartisan safe space in which the challenges raised by life outside the EU could be dissected and discussed, with a view to working out what could be improved, within the bounds of political reality. It was very deliberately a cross-party gathering, convened by one Labour and one Tory peer – Peter Mandelson and Jonathan Hill – both of whom had served as British cabinet ministers and as the UK's commissioner to the European Commission in Brussels. Mandelson held the EU Trade portfolio from 2004 to 2008, while Hill was EU financial services commissioner from November 2014 until June 2016 – when he followed David Cameron's lead and resigned in the light of the UK's vote to leave.

The Ditchley event was a brave attempt to bring Tory and Labour politicians around the same table – from the Conservatives came Michael Gove, a long-standing backer of Brexit, alongside the former Tory leader Michael Howard and the former Tory chancellor Norman Lamont. From the opposition Labour Party came senior members of Keir Starmer's shadow cabinet, including David Lammy, the shadow foreign secretary, and his colleagues covering defence, trade and the Cabinet Office. Senior figures from science and industry were also present, including John Bell, the Regius Professor of Medicine at Oxford University who had led the development of the AstraZeneca Covid-19 vaccine, and the chairs of global companies including the pharmaceutical multinational GSK plc (formerly GlaxoSmithKline) and telecoms giant Vodafone. Supporting the discussion with technical know-how were senior former Whitehall mandarins, including Olly Robbins, who had negotiated Theresa May's failed Brexit deal, and Tom Scholar, the former permanent secretary at the Treasury who was sacked on the orders of Liz Truss at the outset of her disastrous premiership.

It was precisely the kind of broad-based, solutions-focused discussion that has been so often absent from the Brexit debate since 2016. Given that 'in-out' referendums are by their nature binary and Europe had been a politically divisive issue in British politics for decades, it was perhaps naive to think it would be any other way; but almost seven years after the Brexit process began, the Ditchley discussion was a genuine attempt to begin to detoxify that debate. It was based on the premise that rebalancing the conversation away from the political towards the pragmatic will be an essential prerequisite for progress. And that applies to whichever government comes to power after the 2024 general election. Very soon after taking office, the new occupant of Downing Street will need to start to prepare – alongside industry and civil society – for the five-yearly review of the implementation of the EU–UK Trade and Cooperation Agreement (TCA) which is a legal requirement of the deal. If there is political will, the review will provide the first major opportunity to reconsider – on the UK side, at least – what Brexit means, and ask whether the initial sovereignty-at-all-costs approach to leaving the EU pursued by the Johnson government is really the right one.

The reaction to the newspaper report of the Ditchley meeting from a caucus of hard Brexiters was itself indicative of just how difficult this will be, and how much political leadership will be required to move Britain away from the reflexive betrayal narrative that is deployed by those who want to defend the hardest possible Brexit at any cost. 'Secret plan to unravel Brexit' was how the *Daily Mail* characterised the event. Nigel Farage took to social media to warn that 'the full sell-out of Brexit is under way', adding, 'This Tory party never believed in it.' David Frost implied something similar, contending that his Brexit deal didn't 'need 'fixing', it just needed a Conservative government 'to fully and enthusiastically embrace its advantages'. David Jones, the deputy chairman of the European Research Group (ERG) of Eurosceptic Tory MPs that had become the arbiters of Brexit faith during the crucial negotiation years of 2018–20, added darkly that: 'It's hard to believe that closer constitutional links were not on the agenda.'

And what if they were? The idea that moving any closer to the EU is a 'sell-out' of the Brexit ideal is designed to put a straitjacket around any conversation about options for the future. The 'closer constitutional links' of which Jones warned are only sinister if you regard any trade-off on sovereignty as an act of surrender, rather than a balanced calculation of where the national interest lies. We can – and should – argue about the balance of those trade-offs, but such extreme reactions are designed to shut down the space for discussion. Frost's continued assertion that the current Brexit settlement would be brilliant if only it was implemented more enthusiastically ignores the out-turn of the current low-ambition trade deal. Regardless of all the warnings in the economic data, the Brexiters' last argument is that the revolution would surely succeed, if only it was pursued more zealously. And yet for all the talk of 'Brexit opportunities', seven years after Brexit there is still a worrying haziness about what precisely those opportunities might be. General allusions to the UK's prospects in the industries of the future, like gene editing or artificial intelligence, do not amount to a strategy. Unless you count restoring crown stamps on pint pots, of course. This is not to say, as we shall see, that Brexit cannot provide opportunities to do things differently, which may have upsides for some sectors of the economy, but those upsides will always have to be weighed against the downside costs of building back barriers to the market that takes half the UK's trade.

Based on the experience of the first two years properly outside the EU, the numbers are not encouraging. The level of UK goods trade is around 10 per cent to 15 per cent below what it would otherwise have been, according to the Bank of England. Business investment has flatlined since 2016, in part because the uncertainty generated by the prospect of perpetual regulatory upheaval. Brexiters continue to promise this will deliver a future crock of gold at the end of the deregulatory rainbow, but in the meantime, Jonathan Haskel, professor of economics at Imperial College London, and Josh Martin at the Bank of England calculated that Brexit caused a 10 per cent hit to business investment in 2022 which equates to an estimated reduction in GDP of £29 billion – or £1,000 for every household in the UK. And they warned that the pain would not stop there. Their analysis suggested that this figure 'would grow over time unless business investment recovers to where it would have been'.

Brexit is not a problem that will go away if we stop thinking about it. An April 2023 survey by BritishAmerican Business, the transatlantic trade association, showed confidence in the UK falling for three straight years in a row after the EU-UK trade deal came into force. More than two-thirds of US businesses surveyed put fixing post-Brexit trade relations with the EU among their top three priorities to attract investment to the UK. The current trade and investment numbers are surely grounds for a renewed discussion on the balance of Brexit. The current settlement is not – as some Brexiters would have us believe – an expression of the one true Brexit, a static, inviolable covenant that must be defended at all costs. And the polls now suggest the British public knows this perfectly well. When the TCA came into force in early 2021, the public was still split roughly 50:50 about the merits of Brexit, but two years later UK opinion had shifted to nearly 60:40 in favour of rejoining the EU if there was a referendum tomorrow. Drill down into the numbers and it is the loss of confidence in the economics of Brexit among Leave voters that has tipped the overall balance of UK public opinion against the current version of Brexit – even if a majority of Brexiters say they would still vote to leave the EU. Polls also show, across a range of issues, clear majority support for a 'closer' relationship with the EU, even if voters are still uninformed on the trade-offs involved. Those responsible for the current Brexit settlement constantly seek to demonise the notion of compromise, but as the polling guru John Curtice observed, the public is increasingly not with them. 'Rather than looking like an unchallenged "fait accompli",' he wrote on the third anniversary of the UK leaving the EU, 'Brexit now appears to be a subject on which a significant body of voters has had second thoughts.'

But while the public discourse on Brexit is shifting, particularly on the economic consequences of leaving the EU, the political conversation remains paralysed by old fears and animosities. Superficially the atmosphere has improved after Sunak's landing of the Windsor Framework which passed the Commons with a thumping majority and exposed the fact that the once-powerful ERG no longer has the political heft to dictate terms on Brexit.

But both Labour and Conservatives still shy away from the fundamentals of Brexit – the costs it inflicts and the choices it presents. Having seen Boris Johnson romp home in the 2019 general election on the back of a 'Get Brexit Done' agenda, the Labour Party has deliberately closed off any discussion of Brexit that risks accusations that it is once again betraying the wishes of the Leave voters in its former 'Red Wall' heartlands.

In the final days of his premiership in July 2022, as Boris Johnson defended the record of his government, it was to Brexit that he immediately returned, taunting Keir Starmer at the dispatch box for trying to 'overturn the will of the people' during the Theresa May era and reminding him that the outcome was the biggest Tory election victory since 1987, smashing down the Labour 'Red Wall', and turning 'Redcar bluecar'. And it was all down to Brexit, said Johnson. 'Some people will say, as I leave office, that this is the end of Brexit,' he added, pausing for effect. 'Listen to the deathly hush on the Opposition Benches! [That] the Leader of the Opposition and the deep state will prevail in their plot to haul us back into alignment with the EU as a prelude to our eventual return. We on this side of the House will prove them wrong, won't we?'

A full nine months after Johnson left office, and despite the debacle of the Truss premiership, the reaction to the news of the cross-party Ditchley meeting was straight out of the same playbook – to stoke the fear that 'the rejoiners and the revengers' were plotting to reverse the result of the 2016 referendum. But as the worm of public opinion continues to turn, there should be less and less reason for Keir Starmer to maintain a 'deathly hush' over Brexit. He has made clear that he will not look to rejoin the EU, the single market or a customs union with the EU. This shuts down large areas of potentially profitable discussion about where Brexit could go. But still, with the right political leadership, even its current self-limiting position still leaves space to sell a better Brexit than we have now. Because those very same 'Red Wall' manufacturing heartlands that Johnson was so jubilant about stealing from Labour face some of the biggest potential downsides of Brexit. The industries that support a disproportionate number of the best-paying jobs in those communities – automotive, chemical, advanced manufacturing – are the ones most exposed by leaving the EU single market. If Labour is committed to reviving those places, and reducing the economic headwinds facing the UK, why take re-entering a customs union with the EU and more profound regulatory alignment off the table? Because as the Resolution Foundation observed in their June 2023 report 'Trading Up' the alternative is to accept that the UK advanced manufacturers – from chemicals to spacecraft – will gradually fall out of the complex EU supply chains that sustain them. Over time higher- productivity, higher-wage advanced manufacturing will be supplanted by lower-productivity, lower wage manufacturing. The total amount of activity will remain, but the jobs will be less productive and less well-paid. At some point a future government will have to ask itself whether it is happy to leave UK manufacturing (which itself supports investment, research and professional services) to degrade over time, or if it wants to intervene to arrest its looming, Brexit-induced structural decline. The fate of the car industry is an early harbinger of what is to come in other sectors. The first step has to be to introduce honesty into the political conversation and level with voters in areas where manufacturing is economically important – like the Midlands and the North – that Brexit is making them poorer. It is eating away at the future prospects of their children. And it isn't going to stop.

So as the economic costs of Brexit pile up, it's worth asking: who exactly is betraying whom if we refuse to examine more deeply what can be done to improve things? The divisive political legacy of Brexit remains, but the challenge for a future Labour government – or a Conservative government, were it to pivot to a more moderate brand of politics – will be to begin to reframe the discussion around Brexit as a question of economics, not politics or ideology. Even if neither political party is prepared to take radical steps to reduce the economic drag caused by Brexit, then internalising the challenges presented by Brexit is the first step to developing industrial and trade policy to better battle those self-inflicted headwinds. Improving the current TCA is not about 'selling out' Brexit, but about delivering better jobs, a more stable investment climate and greater opportunities to live, work and collaborate with our European neighbours. In truth, nothing was on the agenda at Ditchley, other than the rejection of dogmatism and simplism. Nobody present, Leaver or Remainer, was asked to check their passions and beliefs at the door – and nor did they – but they were asked to come with an open mind and a positive outlook. Indeed, rejoining the EU was explicitly off the agenda. Instead, participants were asked to tackle a much trickier and more pressing question: 'How can we move from the current mix of antagonism and nostalgia to excitement about what the future could bring for the UK and for Europe?'

That is the question to which we now turn.

IO

Rejoin, Resign or Rethink

When the UK voted to leave the EU it faced a range of choices about the shape of its future relationship with Brussels. Theresa May, after a lot of dithering, settled on a relatively high-alignment deal for EU–UK goods trade in order to protect existing UK industries and avoid a return to a hard border in Northern Ireland. It was based around effectively remaining in a customs union with the EU and following a common rulebook for goods trade. The May deal ultimately fell between two stools: too hard for MPs who wanted a very close 'Norway-style' arrangement that kept the UK inside the EU single market; too soft for Brexit purists who demanded the repatriation of undiluted UK sovereignty from Brussels. May's failure to secure her political position at the 2017 general election and then sell her vision for Brexit led to her downfall and opened the door for Boris Johnson, backed by the most hard-line Eurosceptics in the Conservative Party. As we have seen, Johnson delivered a much cleaner break with Brussels, exiting the single market, the customs union and resisting Brussels' attempts to get the UK to sign up to deep 'level playing field' provisions that would have opened up more friction-free access to the EU's single market. The result was greater independence from the EU, but a much more onerous and politically divisive trade border in the Irish Sea and costly frictions for traders operating between Great Britain and the EU. For services, which is a major part of the UK economy, Johnson's trade deal provided very little indeed.

But despite Johnson's promise to 'Get Brexit Done', it is important to remember that the full range of Brexit choices for the UK has not gone away. The politics of Brexit may be blocked until the next UK general election in 2024, but there is nothing that says future governments must be permanently wedded to the Brexit status quo. Of course, any shift in arrangements will need to be negotiated with Brussels. And if the UK wants to move closer to the EU, then the same inescapable trade-offs remain: greater rights come with greater obligations. Ultimately, the EU–UK relationship can, and will, evolve. The full spectrum of relationships remains possible – from moving closer, including applying to rejoin the EU as a member state, to seeking an even more distant relationship than at present.

Can't We Just Rejoin the EU?

The reality, in a world of light and shade, is likely to be something in between. While the simple answer to the question 'what to do about Brexit?' might be 'rejoin the EU', that isn't going to happen any time soon, not least because both the Conservatives and Labour are ruling it out. Superficially, opinion polls show a majority of the country would vote to rejoin, but look deeper into the data and it is clear that unhappiness with the way that the UK's exit has been conducted thus far is not actually the same thing as wanting to rejoin the EU. Voters, like their politicians, tend to be cakeist when it comes to Europe. So while polls now often show voters say they want a 'closer' relationship with the EU, they also don't want a return to freedom of movement and are generally wary of 'taking dictation' from Brussels, except in some areas where there is clear economic advantage or the safety of the nation is at stake. And even if the UK could convince countries like France to let us back in, Britain could not expect to be able to cherry-pick the terms of its relationship with Brussels as, ironically enough, it did during the days of membership. All the opt-outs and rebates that successive prime ministers won from Brussels would not be on the table. Rejoining would almost certainly mean the UK committing to adopt the euro and, at some point in the future, quite possibly taking on some of the debt of other EU countries. For now, none of that is politically realistic and any talk of rejoining is guaranteed to plunge British politics into a fresh round of bitterness and recrimination, leading to further investment-sapping uncertainty. So while a return to EU membership cannot be ruled out many years hence – as older generations die off, younger, more pro-EU voters may take a different view – but it is not part of the foreseeable future.

The Norway Option

What, then, about the so-called 'Norway Option' or 'rejoining the single market'? That's a solution often advanced by Remain voters who simply want the Brexit headache to go away, but accept that fully rejoining is currently unrealistic. We have been here before. During the early debates over what form Brexit should take in 2018, a cross-party group of MPs suggested that the UK should adopt a 'Norway for Now' position, where the UK honoured the Brexit vote but took only an incremental step back from full membership, while it considered its options. But that ship has now sailed. The current debate is no longer about the size of the step *down* from full EU membership, as it was back in 2018, but the extent to which the current relationship can be beefed *up*, off the relatively low base of the TCA.

The reality is that replicating Norway's relationship with the EU would also prove deeply problematic for a country of the size and diplomatic heft of the UK. As a member of the European Economic Area (which also comprises Iceland and Liechtenstein) Norway accepts the 'four freedoms' of the EU – goods, capital, services and people – in exchange for untrammelled access to the EU single market. But Norway has no formal say over the laws and regulations that govern that market, being offered merely a consultative role in their formation. In practice, that means sucking up and implementing into national law large areas of EU single market legislation, including consumer protection, company law, environmental protection and social policy. Between the creation of the EEA in 1994 and the UK's vote to leave in 2016 more than 5,000 new legal acts were incorporated into the EEA Agreement, either as annexes or protocols. Consider all the disagreements of the last seven years over accepting EU laws and it's hard to see how this arrangement would create a politically stable post-Brexit future for the UK.

Norway sits inside the EU single market for services –

including financial services. Is it realistic to think that any British government would allow the City to be a passive rule-taker from EU financial regulators, without having a seat at the table where those regulations were agreed? Norway also makes hefty financial contributions to EU programmes, and accepts the free movement of people, which polls suggest is not something that would currently win popular support in the UK. Supporters of the Norway arrangement often point to 'Article 112' of the EEA Agreement which gives members an 'emergency brake' on free movement if the government can demonstrate that it gives rise to 'serious economic, societal or environmental difficulties of a sectorial or regional nature'. This test has hitherto proved impossible to meet and no one lobbying for a Norway-style relationship should expect it would be met in the future. In practice, a 'Norway' deal means accepting freedom of movement of people. Despite post-Brexit labour market shortages, UK public opinion would need to move further before a return to free movement would become a politically viable proposition for either of the main political parties.

Ultimately, the EEA model works for Norway because it is a small, exceedingly wealthy country whose exports to the EU are dominated by a few products, notably oil and gas. Even then, rule-taking from Brussels causes some political friction in Norway. But for the UK, a country with a permanent seat on the UN Security Council, a globally significant financial centre, the fit is very much less obvious. Signing up to a Norway-style agreement would amount to an act of capitulation. As Professors John Erik Fossum and Hans Petter Graver at the University of Oslo wrote in *Squaring the Circle on Brexit: Could the Norway Model Work?* back in 2018: 'The UK is unlikely to end up balancing state sovereignty, national democracy and market access in a manner similar to Norway.' Nothing that has happened in the last five years suggests they were fundamentally wrong in that assessment.

If not Norway, then What?

So if the UK is not going to rejoin the EU and is not prepared to resign itself to Norway's rule-taking relationship with Brussels, then what? The answer is that there needs to be a fundamental *rethink* both about the UK's relationship with Europe, but also the challenges that now confront us at home. This cannot be a passive exercise that dodges the genuinely hard choices that flow from a decision to erect barriers to our largest export market. Given all the animosity that Brexit has caused, it might be tempting to opt for the quiet life, muddling along and hoping that businesses will simply get used to the frictions imposed by the existing deal. A new prime minister taking office in 2024 might, understandably, be nervous about the risk of having their policy programme immediately hijacked by a return to old arguments over Brexit. But this is too defensive a way of looking at it. Handled correctly, it should be possible to carefully capitalise on the public appetite for change on Brexit if it is framed as a route to delivering economic benefits. Polling in June 2023 by Deltapoll for the Tony Blair Institute found that, when asked to consider the UK and EU's future relationship on a 10-15 year time horizon, 78 per cent of voters said they wanted a closer relationship – either rejoining the EU, re-entering the EU single market or seeking a closer trade and security relationship more generally. As Blair himself summed it up in an article in late 2022: 'It is what it is. There are ways to fix the relationship. It is crucial it is fixed. It can be done without overturning the Brexit decision. So: do it and move on.'

This is why the next Brexit discussion needs to be resolutely forward-looking and focused on addressing the growing economic dissatisfaction with Brexit, with shifts in policy framed clearly within those terms. In any case, a coherent, non-dogmatic future strategy for the UK that combines an industrial policy with net zero ambitions, economic security and trade policy will naturally tend towards closer links with Europe. Brexit was never all about the economy, but addressing the negative economic impacts is the least contentious route towards stabilising the future relationship with the EU. The fact that Brexit is judged to be a failure by a growing number of British voters may also open a space for a broader conversation about the merits of the EU and the value of the cultural, historical and social ties that Brexit has so suddenly constricted. Perhaps absence may make British hearts grow a little fonder of the EU. That still doesn't mean it will be easy. To date, both Conservative and Labour politicians have preferred to skate over the true extent of Britain's Brexit predicament, deflecting reality with banal generalisations or wildly optimistic projections for the UK's potential in future industries.

After delivering his December 2022 budget statement mopping up the mess left by Liz Truss's market-melting 'KamiKwasi' budget, the chancellor Jeremy Hunt was asked about how to address the economic downsides of Brexit. He simply stated that he had 'great confidence' that the UK 'will find outside the single market we are able to remove the vast majority of the trade barriers that exist between us and the EU'. Given the Conservative Party's red lines on Brexit, it is not at all clear what that confidence is based upon, other than wishful thinking. The review of the TCA in 2026 will not be a something-for-nothing negotiation, even if the diplomatic mood music has improved thanks to the Windsor Framework and the more conciliatory style of Rishi Sunak. The UK knows this from the experience of the 2017–20 negotiations, when there were no freebies on offer. David Lammy, the shadow foreign secretary, was only marginally more convincing than Hunt when delivering a speech at Chatham House in January 2023. He reiterated that with Labour the UK would 'not rejoin the EU, the single market or the customs union' while promising that – within those red lines – there is 'real progress we can make . . . to fix the Tories' bad Brexit' and 'increase trade with Europe'.

To a point. But merely tinkering with the TCA within those red lines will not transform the UK's trade prospects; if the Frost deal is the equivalent of a Ford Fiesta, then even operating it at maximum revolutions will not turn it into the trading Ferrari that was the EU single market. To think so would be to misunderstand the structural nature of barriers to trade caused by Brexit. And yet doing nothing isn't an option either, because it's wrong to assume that conditions will gradually improve as businesses continue to adjust to life outside the EU. Quite possibly, the opposite is the case. When the Brexit trade deal came into force, there was a foundational 'stock' of trading relationships in which both sides had already invested. Bigger businesses with production already set up swallowed the reduced margins and higher costs, but it's likely that they will wind up some facilities at the end of their life, at which point the logic will point to investing in new production in the EU. As that March 2023 report into post-Brexit exporting conditions by the Institute of Directors warned, EU companies are going cold on the UK: 'If firms within the EU already have access to markets within a customs union which do not require extensive documentation, proof of origin, labelling, and costs, why would they expend resource on businesses which do?' This is what should be causing real concern. As an EU member, companies built factories and invested in the UK in part because it provided a friction-free entrepôt to the largest consumer market on the planet, alongside a precious combination of access to flexible labour markets, strong research and development skills, dependable regulation and engagement with highly integrated EU supply chains. Brexit has hobbled that model.

The question now is how far – short of re-entering the EU single market – the UK can move in order to fix it.

II

Resetting with Europe

Before British negotiators sit down with their European counterparts in 2026 to try to improve upon the TCA, a concerted diplomatic effort will be needed to repair relations both with the EU institutions and European capitals. The years of bruising Brexit talks – where at times senior UK politicians saw engineering confrontation with Brussels as a badge of honour – have eroded trust between Europe and the UK in a manner that will not be quick and easy to repair. The damage runs far beyond the usual scars that come from the cut-and-thrust of a hard-fought trade negotiation. Divorce negotiations are always bitter affairs, but the Brexit process has raised persistent questions about whether the UK can now be relied upon to be the pragmatic force in European affairs for which it long held a reputation.

Over the last seven years the UK has frequently failed to keep it civil. EU diplomats at the Conservative Party Conference in Manchester in 2021 sat in the front row of the main speech hall and listened to David Frost describe the UK's 50 years of EU membership as a 'long bad dream', which felt gratuitous, even by the standards of a domestic political party shindig. But it fitted a pattern. In 2018 Jeremy Hunt compared the EU's handling of Brexit to the former Soviet Union punishing a satellite state for trying to leave the bloc. At the height of the Withdrawal Agreement negotiations in 2019 Steve Barclay, then Brexit secretary, went to Madrid and gave a speech in which he appeared to threaten the future of the Spanish tourism industry and question whether Ireland would have access to sufficient medicines in the event of a 'no-deal' exit. At one point in the talks Johnson compared himself to the Incredible Hulk comic-book character. 'The madder Hulk gets, the stronger Hulk gets,' he told an interviewer in September 2019. Guy Verhofstadt, then the Brexit lead for the European Parliament, replied on Twitter that 'even by Trumpian standards' the Hulk comparison was 'infantile'.

Frost and co. convinced themselves that such a boorish approach to diplomacy was the only way to make headway in Brussels, even though their belief was never borne out by the results. In fact, as Michel Barnier's senior aide Stefaan De Rynck wrote in his account of the talks, *Inside the Deal*, deliberately getting up European noses had precisely the opposite effect and 'galvanised the EU's unity on crucial occasions'. Ultimately, as Charles Grant, the director of the Centre for European Reform think tank and one of the best-connected Brits in Brussels, wrote after Frost's resignation in December 2021, the UK's embrace of the 'thump 'em school of diplomacy' just made everyone in Europe exhausted and cross. As he correctly observed: 'Frost made himself an extraordinarily unpopular figure in Brussels and in EU capitals.'

But while diplomatic barbs and brickbats might be relatively quickly forgotten – personalities pass, memories fade – threats to renege on international agreements within months of signing them leave potential future treaty partners with much deeper misgivings. Post-Brexit Conservative governments twice tabled legislation designed to unilaterally rip up their freely given international treaty commitments over Northern Ireland. Conservative UK prime ministers, including Sunak, have also repeatedly said they would be open to withdrawing from the European Convention on Human Rights – the same treaty which underpins both the Good Friday Agreement in Northern Ireland and the criminal justice sections of the TCA. The scars of Brexit run deep. EU capitals watched incredulously as Boris Johnson was unanimously overruled by the judges of the UK Supreme Court for illegally closing down the British Parliament and then, after being forced to return home early from the annual UN General Assembly, was utterly unrepentant on his return.

Johnson's apparently cosy relationship with Donald Trump – who lionised Johnson when he took office in 2019, breaking into a speech to say 'they call him "Britain Trump" and people are saying that's a good thing' – further poisoned the well of trust in Europe. Now both out of office, neither Trump nor

Johnson appear to have given up their ambitions and are likely to loom large over future governments in the US and UK whatever the outcomes of elections in 2024. The coincidence of the Brexit vote and the election of Trump in 2016 had already deepened the sense that Brexit was an expression of a populist, nationalist movement that was, at the time, threatening to undo the EU – with Trump cheering from the sidelines. Those clouds passed relatively quickly, but they left a bitterness in Brussels. And it doesn't take much to summon the aftertaste.

Any UK leader who now seeks to re-engage with Europe will therefore have to work diligently to counter the nagging worry that British politics has been permanently altered by Brexit. From a European perspective, diplomats frequently caution that any future agreements with the UK will need to be insulated against the risk that the UK reverts back to the populist pugilism of the Johnson years. This is not about individual personalities, but the fear of a structural shift in the UK polity. Sunak's laudable efforts to find constructive solutions to the dispute over the implementation of the Northern Ireland Protocol were welcomed in Brussels, but the latent anti-EU forces in British politics have not disappeared. If Sunak wins in 2024, they will still be there, restricting his room for manoeuvre.

Equally, if Starmer wins, particularly with a slender parliamentary majority, he will still need to contend with Tory Brexiters fomenting opposition to any attempt to forge a rapprochement with Europe. If the Conservative Party shifts further to the right in response to a heavy electoral defeat, then the UK's first-past-the-post electoral system means the risk of the Brexiters' return to power in 2029 will be a negative factor in TCA review negotiations due to start in 2026. In that scenario, the EU may ask itself why it should bother going the extra mile when in three years' time an incoming Conservative might take everything back to square one. This is not to say that it is not worth making the effort – indeed it is absolutely vital that proper relations are restored – but merely to warn that the installation of a more pro-EU Labour government in Westminster will not suddenly see Brussels flick a diplomatic switch and restore the status quo ante.

To his credit, since coming to office Sunak started to reset relations with both Brussels and EU capitals, including Paris,

Berlin, Warsaw and Dublin. The diplomatic outreach, which had initially began under Liz Truss, has not gone unnoticed. As the negotiations over Northern Ireland progressed, diplomats who spent five years rolling their eyes at the politics of Johnson, Truss and Frost, suddenly spoke warmly of 'shared ambitions'. The conflict in Ukraine has also helped remind both sides of their shared strategic priorities. The UK was right to attend the inaugural meeting of the French-led European Political Community in Prague in October 2022, along with the 27 EU leaders and 17 other countries from the wider region, including Ukraine, Turkey, Albania and Switzerland. It was a largely symbolic gesture but one that sent a message that the post-Brexit UK does wish to re-engage with Europe.

Sunak, who needs better French support to address the small boats crisis in the Channel, also worked to patch things up with Emmanuel Macron, accepting an invitation to a summit in Paris in March 2023. And in a calculated compliment to Europe, the new King Charles III also chose France and Germany for his first overseas state visit. There has also been substance as well as symbolism. Coordinating economic sanctions following the Ukraine crisis provided a genuine pretext for EU–UK cooperation and, with little fanfare, the UK has signed up to a couple of small EU-led regional forums. In November 2022 the UK signed up to an EU defence programme, the PESCO Military Mobility, to facilitate the movement of troops and military hardware across the EU – not a massive deal, since the US, Canada and Norway had already joined in 2021, but notable all the same. And in December 2022 the UK signed a memorandum of understanding with the North Seas Energy Cooperation, an increasingly important regional forum for renewable energy in the North Sea which is co-chaired by the European Commission. These steps send the signal that the UK does want to move on.

Still, that cannot instantly make up for the massive diplomatic deficit that Brexit leaves behind. Every three months, come what may, all the leaders of the 27 EU member states travel to Brussels for the quarterly European Council summit. The discussions can often be long-winded, frustrating and go long into the night, but they also provide a regular opportunity for EU leaders to build personal relationships with each other, while their officials work behind the scenes to triangulate policy differences. Those personal relationships between officials – the so-called 'sherpas' of international affairs – are themselves essential, particularly in a crisis. When an invasion comes, or when there is a meltdown in the bond markets, these are the people who keep the diplomatic plumbing running smoothly. When British officials in the Treasury or the Foreign Office pick up the phone to counterparts in Europe, it makes a huge difference when they have a personal connection with the voice on the end of the line. Brexit means the UK is now outside these corridors of power, no longer axiomatically copied in on all the official paperwork as it circulates around Brussels. And the longer it goes on, the more relations will atrophy as officials who had built up a stock of relationships pre-Brexit retire or take their contacts books off into the private sector. Without that in-built contact time, the next generation of British diplomats will never enjoy the access and clout enjoyed by their predecessors.

Brexit also impacts other strategic relationships, sapping the UK's wider credibility, including in Washington, which can no longer use the UK as a diplomatic hinge with Brussels. Since Brexit that role has visibly diminished while Washington has simultaneously deepened institutional ties with the EU. Since 2021 the US and the EU have established a new 'Defense and Future Forum' and a joint 'Trade and Technology Council' (TTC) at which the EU and US are discussing security, defence and common approaches to global issues like data management and artificial intelligence. In December 2022, for example, the TTC agreed to create a common standard for heavy-duty electric vehicle charging and launched an early warning system for issues in semiconductor supply chains. As the UK Parliament's Foreign Affairs Committee warned in late 2022, this initiative between the world's two regulatory powerhouses 'risks sidelining the UK', with the UK 'becoming a "rule-taker" rather than a "rule-maker"'. The UK has bilateral forums with the US on technology, but officials rightly fret that the country should be looking for a seat at the TTC table; and unless it can make the case to be included, the UK risks – as Carnegie Europe warned in their 2021 report on the future of EU–UK foreign policy after Brexit, *Rivals or Partners* – 'remaining outside the room where decisions with implications for its economic and technological interests are made'. As one senior UK security official put it to me: 'The US administration forgets us quite a lot now, apart from on pure defence stuff. Because the US increasingly sees the world through an EU–US lens, and now when they think of Europe, they don't think of the UK – just like when the EU thinks about America, it doesn't think much about Canada.' An EU official that co-ordinates the EU's external security arrangements made a very similar observation to me, but from a different perspective: 'There are structures that mean I speak to US counterparts almost every day, but after all these years the UK is suddenly not there, except on an ad hoc basis. The diplomatic apparatus just doesn't exist.'

There is no instant or complete fix for this – unless the UK rejoins the EU its prime minister will not be attending European Councils – but there are concrete steps the UK could take to start to limit the diplomatic damage. In her 2017 Lancaster House speech Theresa May promised to 'work closely with our European allies in foreign and defence policy' even though the UK was leaving the EU itself. A Command Paper published in 2018 set out plans for an ambitious seven-point EU–UK partnership agreement covering foreign, defence and development policy that promised 'regular dialogues', joint humanitarian missions, defence capability development, intel-ligence-sharing and cooperation on strategic space projects. Negotiations got under way to sketch out such an agreement, but struggled in part because the EU feared that the UK was looking to leverage its defence and security prowess to gain cherry-picked access to the EU single market. That was a tactical mistake on the part of the UK, since it riled Brussels and member states, who viewed the security and trade files as utterly separate and were determined to keep them that way. When Boris Johnson came along, that became a moot point, because the idea of building such a broad foreign policy frame-work agreement was dropped. (The fact that the top body in the TCA is called the 'Partnership Council' is an accidental leftover of that previous attempt at deeper cooperation – 'We wanted to call this a "partnership agreement" but Johnson didn't, but only ever got around to changing the cover page,' recalls one senior EU official.)

The UK should now look to revive it – and explicitly not as leverage to improve the current trade deal, but as a sincere expression that the UK is still determined to make good on Theresa May's original promise, because it is worth it, on its own terms. After years when UK officials were discouraged from reaching out to Europe by politicians who were determined to do nothing that could be construed as moving back into the orbit of the EU, it is time to work vigorously to restore what Peter Mandelson has called the 'habits of cooperation'. The UK could even try to create some new diplomatic architecture – a European Security Council – that can create pretexts to get the UK back in the room with EU leaders at least on an annual basis. A new strategic dialogue with Europe could also provide a platform to coordinate on issues of shared interest, like climate change, energy security, biosecurity issues (recalling the pandemic), as well as sanctions enforcement. That top-level engagement also needs to be matched by a serious new commitment to the UK Mission (in effect, embassy) in Brussels. A beefed-up ambassadorial appointment in Brussels, perhaps even an American-style appointment of a figure who has the ear of the prime minister, might also help to open doors.

These may yield talking-shops in the first instance, but that in itself has value in a world where the UK is now too often outside the door in Europe. Stronger bilateral relations with key capitals – Paris, Berlin, Madrid, Rome and Warsaw, for example – are also imperative. As will be continuing to build on the UK's role underpinning Nordic–Baltic security. Not because the UK should seek to 'divide and rule' between EU member states (the 2016–20 Brexit negotiations showed this is always counterproductive) but because warmer relations in key capitals will be important in getting influential EU member states to convince the European Commission to take a less Manichean and defensive line towards engagement with the UK on other issues. There are also commitments that the UK government could consider as a concrete expression of their determination to build a functional post-Brexit diplomatic architecture.

A defence agreement might, for example, enable the UK to contribute to EU peacekeeping missions abroad, like Operation Althea – officially, the European Union Force Bosnia and Herzegovina. That might only mean sending a handful of UK advisers, but it would be a show of regional solidarity. When an EU member, the UK mostly worked to thwart efforts at intra-EU defence cooperation, but with the UK no longer applying the brakes, Brussels is becoming an increasingly significant player in defence spending and procurement. Going deeper, the UK could consider following Norway and contribute to the EU's €5.6 billion Peace Facility which has helped fund arms shipments to Ukraine, and the European Defence Agency, which coordinates defence projects in Europe and which the US and the EU proposed a joint cooperation agreement in February 2023. There would be political and financial trade-offs to these kinds of collaborations – British politicians tend to want to put Union flags on British military aid – but they would have to be weighed against the upside of building a deeper strategic relationship in the neighbourhood.

In short, it's time to move on. The experience of the first Brexit negotiations – for both sides – might lead to a cautious approach to rebuilding the relationship after the damage caused during the Johnson era. But there are also reasons to believe that history does not have to repeat itself. Compared to 2016 the EU is a visibly more self-confident organisation, having been through the collective challenges posed by the 2015 migrant exodus and eurozone banking crisis, the era of Trumpian populism and then the Covid-19 and Ukraine energy crises. The entire organisation is no longer in quite the same defensive crouch that was triggered by Trump, Brexit and the rise of Euroscepticism in France and Italy. By the time the trade deal comes up for its five-year review in 2026 it will also be ten years since the Brexit vote, and the generation of leaders that made the political weather in that era, like Angela Merkel, will have moved on. Only Emmanuel Macron remains, and his second term will expire in the spring of 2027. The bureaucracy in Brussels has also shifted somewhat and is no longer quite so dominated by the stereotypical French lawyers who specialise in thwarting the Brits, even if EU industrial policy thinking is still driven by Paris. Instead there are more eastern European diplomats from countries like Poland, the Baltics, Romania and Bulgaria who are generally better-disposed to the UK. At the same time, the Ukraine war and the global energy crisis has reminded everyone that there are bigger things to worry about than Brexit. There are fresh handholds emerging for the UK in its post-Brexit relations with Europe; we should grasp them.

12

Fixing the TCA: Go Large or Stay Home?

The first two rounds of Brexit negotiations – the 2019 Withdrawal Agreement, or 'divorce deal', and then the subsequent trade negotiation in 2020 – were a bruising experience for the British state. From the start, a big part of the problem was a chronic lack of preparation and strategic thinking. During the 2016 referendum campaign David Cameron forbade diplomats and civil servants from making preparations for the possibility that there might be a vote to leave, with the result that when the unthinkable (to Cameron, at least) happened, Whitehall found itself at a standing start. Even then, officials recall that in the months after the referendum – as the debate raged over when to serve the Article 50 notice and start the European Commission's clock ticking on the two-year departure process – time was wasted. The creation of a separate Whitehall department for Exiting the European Union, far from aiding decision-making, spawned a competing power centre with Downing Street that just became a distraction. Theresa May's Europe adviser, Raoul Ruparel, recalled that part of the reason that May delivered such an incoherent jumble of ideas in her disastrous 2016 party conference speech was the lack of serious policy work in the run-up to the decision to trigger Article 50. 'The nine months up until the triggering of Article 50 was largely wasted in terms of actually preparing and getting ready,' he told the UK in a Changing Europe's Brexit archive which conducted interviews with many of the key players in the Brexit story. 'You can argue whether Article 50 was triggered too early or not. In the end, those nine months were quite a lot of time. You could get quite a lot of stuff done in that period, if you'd used it properly, but we didn't.'

If the UK wants to get third time lucky with Brussels, then the mistakes of the original negotiation must not be repeated. The first step is an end to the magical thinking of the May era, when the cabinet came up with clever schemes to solve their own differences (like the dual-track customs system that featured in the Chequers Plan of summer 2018) that were never going to be negotiable with Brussels. And then Johnson's pell-mell trade negotiation in 2020 in which the difficult trade-offs over access to the EU single market were resolved largely by lowering the ambition for the deal. As a result, the concerns of the business community (who actually did the trading) were often actively ignored, while a broader discussion with the public about the shape of the UK's relationship with Europe was never initiated. The second step must be to hold that discussion about the future. There is an opportunity for the UK to do things differently when the TCA comes up for review after 2026, but it will require political courage and strategic clarity of thought from the outset. Therefore, the first question the prime minister of the day must ask themselves is: 'Is the TCA implementation review just an exercise in technocratic tinkering, or is the British government prepared to try and make it an inflection point for a deeper and more comprehensive re-engagement with the EU?'

Fudging the answer to that question, which is the natural habit of politicians, would be a mistake. The last seven years have cratered the relationship between investors and the government. Businesses and their representative trade bodies are already drawing up shopping lists of requests for improvements to the existing deal. Stringing them along with fig-leaf consultations will only deepen the frustrations over dealing with governments that have sapped the confidence of British managers to invest in their businesses. Drinks parties at Number 10 or conversations over coffee with the prime minister's business adviser just serve as cosmetic exercises in 'making people feel heard' but, if they do not materially impact on policy, they will only reignite resentments. Indeed, it would be better to be candid that the current TCA has inherent limitations and that there is no political appetite to do what is necessary to shift the dial sufficiently to deliver meaningful improvements. At least then business has certainty and can make plans accordingly – even if, on the evidence so far, that means lower investment, reduced trade openness, lower productivity and a reduced ability overall to attract high-end skills to the UK.

But if the decision is to try to do something substantial to deepen first diplomatic and then trade ties, then – as Ruparel observed ahead of the 2020 trade deal negotiation – the UK needs to have 'a clear idea about how it wants the negotiations to run, and get Whitehall ready to deliver its plan'. Because you can bet your last euro that the European negotiators will be prepared. The vast Brussels bureaucracy will grind into gear and produce neatly tabulated charts of where EU interests lie and where the European Commission might give ground – if it could obtain the right concession from the British side. In reality, given the relative sizes of the two economies, the UK will remain as the *demandeur* in the negotiation – the UK accounts for only 6 per cent of the EU's total trade with the rest of the world, while the EU is nearly 50 per cent of the UK's – but with the right offer, allied to the right atmospherics, useful improvements could still be achieved. Those arguing that the politics will be too hard, that this should be a 'second term issue' if Labour are elected in 2024, overlook the fact that that would mean five more years in which supply chains will re-orientate, investment will drain away and diplomatic and people-to-people relationships between the EU and the UK will continue to atrophy.

But to be successful in beginning the EU reboot, the UK will need clearly defined ambitions for which it has created broad public backing based around improved trading links and stronger ties for students, young people, artists and scientific collaboration. That public support for a pragmatic new settlement, for which it appears there is support in the polls, will be important in framing the negotiation both at home and in Brussels. The successful negotiations over the Northern Ireland Protocol showed that the European Commission can be moved to make concessions when it finds itself on the wrong side of public arguments. But more important will be domestic political outreach to build a narrative around the coming negotiation that moves the discussion away from the bitter partisanship of the early Brexit years. Labour's decision to offer their up-front backing to Rishi Sunak over the Windsor Framework for Northern Ireland – having ultimately refused to back Theresa May's deal in 2018 – demonstrated that the highly partisan political debate on Brexit is moving on. It also showed that the arbiters of Brexit do not always have to be the small coterie of purists that for too long held a monopoly of wisdom on what is acceptable.

One way of reframing the debate away from party-political animosities would be to institute a cross-party, evidence-gathering exercise to kick-start a national debate on the future of EU–UK relations. It's a debate that should have been held in 2016 before exit negotiations began, but in the rawness of the referendum aftermath that proved impossible. Of course, the UK is not starting from a clean slate – what's done is done – but with the most livid scars from the Brexit debate now starting to fade, such a conversation is potentially possible. Much of the work has already been done in parliamentary select committees and by business and civil society groups, but their voices have mostly been carried off in the prevailing political winds. That public outreach needs to be allied with genuine and deep consultation with business and civil society – from businesses to trades unions, farmers to fishermen, cultural and conservation groups – that have a stake in better relations with the EU. Such an exercise must be fundamentally forward-looking, not a score-settling exercise apportioning blame for what has already happened – and specifically very different from a judge-led public inquiry which would be a long-winded and fruitless way of stirring up old animosities. There would be an element of political gamble in setting up such a forum, since it might become a target for naysayers crying 'betrayal' of Brexit, but as the rapprochement over Northern Ireland's situation showed, fatigue is setting in with these arguments both at Westminster and beyond. Well handled, it could become a lightning rod for a new settlement, providing political cover for the silent centre-ground and empowering a new government that is not constrained by the need to defend the failures of the first two negotiations.

Another reason for a broad-based discussion about a new post-Brexit relationship is to socialise both public and politicians to the actual trade-offs that face the UK now we are outside the EU single market. A commission of enquiry into how to revitalise UK–EU relations must not be a thinly veiled exercise in building arguments for rejoining but should seek to find solutions within the broad political parameters laid down by the government of the day. The sensitivities around Brexit politics have led both main parties to sugar the pill of leaving. Compromise has too often been cast in simplistic terms as somehow reneging on the 2016 vote, when in reality Brexit confronts the UK with a world of complex choices that will not be solved by cakeism. Polls consistently show that the public has not really internalised the choices on offer: voters say they want 'better' economic relations with the EU, but they don't want to accept the rulings of the European Court of Justice, regulatory alignment or free movement. To one degree or another, each is a function of the other.

Can the UK sustain a mass-production car industry if it is not in a customs union with the EU (thereby removing the 'rules of origin' issue) – or if it is not dynamically aligned on a host of EU single market standards and regulations from data to the environment? More broadly, in which sectors would the UK benefit from regulatory alignment with the EU? Where might space to diverge pay dividends? If the UK rejoined the EU customs union, what is the opportunity cost in not being able to negotiate free trade deals separately from the EU? What are those deals worth anyway? Should the UK sign a high-alignment veterinary agreement with the EU? If it did so, what would that mean for the UK prospects of signing a free trade deal with the United States? In the current global trade environment, how likely is the UK to secure a trade deal with Washington in any case? If the UK wants to be a 'science super-power' and have the highest growth in the G7 – as Starmer says he does – then how isolated can it afford to be from the advanced market on its doorstep?

Moving the discussion forward will certainly require a conscious break with the absolutist sovereignty-at-all-costs version of Brexit that presents any compromise with Brussels as a sell-out, rather than a conscious decision taken in the UK's political and economic interests. In a globalised world, where the internet creates a virtual world without borders, and where regulation rather than tariffs defines the barriers and opportunities for international trade, sovereignty is never unalloyed. It is a fungible commodity which nation states trade off when they make international agreements they judge to be in their interests – whether signing up to trade agreements, defence pacts or climate mitigation targets. The aversion of a certain section of the Conservative Party towards making these trade-offs with Brussels has warped the debate around Brexit, sometimes with obviously absurd results. (At one point in the 2020 trade negotiations the UK was offering deeper concessions to Japan than it was to the EU.)

It is important to remember that, before Brexit, the Tory Party was not so binary in its dealings with the EU. Just two years before the referendum in 2014, Theresa May, then home secretary, successfully confronted the sovereigntists on her backbenches over the need for the UK to sign up to the European arrest warrant. This was a system that replaced a network of cumbersome national extradition treaties to create a seamless means of sending alleged criminals to face trial in other EU countries. Clearly that cut both ways – the UK could demand the extradition of EU nationals to face trial in Britain, but equally EU countries could force British nationals to be sent to stand trial in France, Greece or Hungary.

May faced down objections from Tory rebels who argued that the European arrest warrant would leave potentially innocent Brits at the mercy of some EU jurisdictions they did not consider to have equivalent protections or standards. But she persuaded the majority of her party otherwise: 'Our guiding principle was and remains that if there is no clear purpose for a European law, there shouldn't be a European law,' she wrote. 'But where we need to cooperate with other member states to fight crime, prevent terrorism and protect the public, we will do so.' In other words, there was a trade-off worth making: sovereignty in exchange for safety. It is telling that the roll-call of 37 Tory rebels that opposed May's decision contains many of the same names that later drove the Brexit debate into such a destructive and self-defeating cul-de-sac – Steve Baker, Andrew Bridgen, William Cash, Bernard Jenkin, Dominic Raab, John Redwood and Jacob Rees-Mogg, to name but a few.

Any move to substantially deepen EU–UK relations is going to require accepting more of these kinds of trade-offs, based on a clear-eyed cost–benefit analysis rather than an allergic rejection of any influence for EU courts over the UK. Even in the current deal, the UK accepts the oversight of the European Court of

Justice when it cooperates with EU agencies and programmes, like the scientific collaboration programme Horizon Europe. And even where European Court of Justice rulings do not have directly applicable effect in the UK, the court's rulings on areas including law enforcement, data exchange or judicial cooperation exert a strong indirect effect. That's because in practice the UK will have to heed the judgments of the court in order to retain access to such schemes, like extradition agreements, or the 'data adequacy decision' under which the EU deems UK data protection rules are essentially equivalent to the EU's. Preserving that decision – which can be withdrawn by the EU Commission unilaterally at short notice – is vital for UK business. It's also worth recalling that as part of the Withdrawal Agreement, the UK agreed that the European Court of Justice had jurisdiction over the citizens' rights elements of the deal, if the UK courts sought clarification on points of EU law. In short, the 'red lines' over the European Court of Justice will need to get pinker for progress to be made.

But if the UK wants to make real progress with Brussels, it will not be enough simply to have a clear-eyed assessment of the UK negotiating objectives, a strong delivery structure in Whitehall and a less allergic attitude to the role of the European Court of Justice. Nor will a diplomatic offensive, however welcome, pay immediate dividends when it comes to improving the Trade and Cooperation Agreement. While all of those things are essential, the reality of any negotiation is that you don't get something for nothing. The UK side needs to ponder deeply what it is prepared to give the EU in order to shift the dial in negotiations. Because while influential figures in the UK are convening high-level meetings at Oxfordshire's Ditchley Park to discuss Brexit, equivalent meetings were not taking place in the chateaux of the Dordogne or the schlosses of Bavaria. Beyond the low-grade irritation caused by the long-running saga over finding a workable deal on Northern Ireland, since the UK–EU trade deal came into force, Brexit is no longer a first-order issue in Brussels.

Indeed, as things stand, the EU might argue the TCA suits them perfectly well: it provides tariff-free access to the UK market for EU goods exporters (the EU runs a goods surplus with the UK) while providing very little assistance for UK service industries, in which the UK runs a surplus with the EU. The UK can take steps to rebalance a deal that, in the first two years of implementation, was deeply asymmetrical. The decision to introduce full border checks on EU imports from October 2024 means that EU exporters to the UK will belatedly start to face some of the same bureaucratic pain that their British counterparts have faced since January 2021. The UK will, of course, have to strike a balance between maintaining free-flowing supply chains to the UK while equalising the bureaucratic pain being felt by both sides.

The EU's enormous size and regulatory heft relative to the UK leaves British business at a constant comparative disadvantage to EU competitors. This risks sapping investment from British industry, from cars to chemicals. The outlook is for life outside the single market to get tougher. Looking to the future, the EU is becoming increasingly aggressive in using the power of its single market to dictate terms globally to exporters. Schemes like the new Carbon Border Adjustment Mechanism (CBAM) – which will require exporters to the EU to show they are not 'importing' carbon by using inputs from less green countries, and pay a tax if they are – risk creating another huge layer of bureaucracy for UK exporters. The EU 'Green Deal' is also filled with new regulations that effectively amount to a 'buy European' strategy. Food and drink manufacturers will find that the EU's Farm to Fork Strategy bans the import of foods grown with certain pesticides or production practices. In short, the onward march of EU regulation will deepen the challenge for many UK sectors outside the EU single market.

To mitigate against these asymmetries the UK will need to consider deep regulatory alignment with the EU, where it makes economic sense for individual sectors and industries. If the UK can accept EU alignment including European Court of Justice oversight in order to extradite criminals, then why not to help its exporters of cars, food and drink or industrial goods? Only if you clung with blind fervour to the binary conception of Brexit, where upsides can only be achieved by diverging from the EU, would you rule out alignment where it palpably makes sense. One example is CBAM – the carbon border tax – that the EU is proposing, which will protect EU producers from imports that are made in countries where pollution is cheap. To enforce the tax, the EU will demand that non-EU exporters produce yet more paperwork to prove their products have paid an equivalent carbon price; if they cannot, they must pay the tax. For UK exporters that will mean yet more of a bureaucratic burden at the EU–UK border. One obvious way round this is to legally link the carbon-pricing systems of the EU and the UK. The independent Centre for Inclusive Trade Policy think tank said in evidence to the Lords that linking the UK and EU schemes would obviate a major potential source of border pain. True, this would mean the UK foregoing discretion in designing its own CBAM scheme and carbon market, but the UK will have to consider whether this was a fair trade-off in order to significantly reduce friction for UK–EU trade – in both directions. The Centre for Inclusive Trade Policy estimated the disadvantages of linking the UK and EU schemes would be 'dwarfed' by the advantages for trade. These are the kinds of decisions that need making, and without ideological preconceptions.

The case for UK regulatory alignment with the EU may well be strong in other sectors of the economy – for example, cars, chemicals, pharmaceuticals, aerospace and industrial goods, agri-food – but each will have to make their own cost–benefit analysis. Of course, it's important to be clear that the UK voluntarily aligning with the EU would not, in itself, deliver friction-free access to the EU single market, even if it would reduce bureaucratic headaches for UK exporters, or UK manufacturers reliant on EU supply chains. What confers preferential access to the EU single market is submitting to the oversight of EU regulators and the jurisdiction of the European Court of Justice. Viewed from Brussels, therefore, a UK decision to voluntarily align would merely be seen as evidence of the EU's single market exerting its inexorable gravitational pull on UK industry. In that sense UK voluntary alignment is a unilateral offer to the EU – but there are those who argue it could provide a stepping stone to winning deeper flexibility from Brussels.

Peter Holmes of the UK Trade Policy Observatory think tank said the TCA contains the mechanisms to enable 'win–win' revisions to reduce trade frictions, including scope for Regulatory Cooperation. 'But the UK must prepare itself to discuss options that will require genuine concessions on the UK side, through public debate and detailed cost–benefit analysis rather than a preference for sovereignty at any cost,' he warns. David Henig, a former UK trade negotiator now at the European Centre for International Political Economy think tank, reaches a similar conclusion in his paper *Building a Mature UK Trade Policy* where he observed the UK is trying to build an independent trade policy just at the moment when the EU, US and China are putting national interest above the previously accepted norms of global trade. His recipe is the same one that business is also arguing for: that UK policy-makers consider 'dynamic alignment where helpful, UK unilateral action where beneficial – for example possibly in financial services – but predictability and competence in all cases'.

One proposal from the Tony Blair Institute advocates that rather than simply aligning on an *ad hoc* basis, the UK should pass domestic legislation binding the government to maintaining high regulatory standards in key areas – for example food safety, labour rights and environmental standards – while following EU rules in sectors where it makes sense to do so. Labour has already said that, if elected, it will seek a veterinary and SPS deal with the EU, which is itself likely to require continuous future alignment with EU rules. Putting those commitments on the UK statute book would have a stabilising effect on the future EU–UK relationship – which is by its nature unstable, since the UK's legislative framework can always be changed by a simple majority in the UK Parliament. It would have the reverse effect of the deeply destabilising Retained EU Law Bill, which threatened to rip up all EU-derived law in a year. As well as giving greater certainty to business and investors, Anton Spisak, a former Whitehall official who worked on previous Brexit negotiations and is now at the Blair Institute, has argued that such a structured, statutory commitment could provide the legal launchpad to transform the ambition of the TCA review. 'A commitment to high standards through the introduction of UK laws would be an important signal to the EU about the future direction of the UK's regulatory model,' he wrote. 'This is a necessary step to unlocking constructive negotiations that could lead to more beneficial trade arrangements.'

After all, the journey must start somewhere. Unless the Labour party's position shifts dramatically, healing the damage caused by Brexit will be a multistage process. It must start with what the

Resolution Foundation characterises as 'defensive' measures designed to protect high-value UK industries like cars, aerospace, medical devices and chemicals that rely on access to integrated EU supply chains. Measures like legally linking EU and UK carbon pricing schemes, but also trying as far as possible to reduce frictions within the parameters of the existing agreements, such as doing an alignment deal on veterinary standards and digitising borders, as a foundation for a deeper realignment. The spectrum of possibilities is looked at in the next chapter. Who is to say where this process could lead five or ten years from now? The Resolution Foundation in its June 2023 report 'Trading Up' goes so far as to posit that, at some point in the future, the UK could seek to duplicate the market access arrangements enjoyed by Northern Ireland for the whole of the UK. It's an idea that will be shouted down as 'cherry picking' in Brussels now, but membership of the EU single market for goods was essentially the deal negotiated by Theresa May as part of her 'backstop' arrangements for Northern Ireland. As the report observes: 'A trade strategy is not just about what is on the table right now – it is also about laying the groundwork for future deals that align with the broader needs of the UK economy. The precedent of the Northern Ireland Protocol and the existence of mutual gains for the UK and the EU make a new goods trading arrangement feasible at some point, were a UK Government were to prioritise it as a core component of its trade strategy.' For now, the most important thing is that the UK should have the aspiration.

This might feel like the UK throwing itself on the mercy of Brussels, but given the bad blood of the last seven years and the imbalance of incentives to improve the TCA, the UK will need to do something to signal it is taking a fundamentally different tack to previous post-Brexit governments. This is not a counsel of despair but a recognition that the UK needs to be realistic in its ambitions and the structure of its economic relations with the EU. If a new British prime minister arrives in Brussels with a shopping list of UK improvements soon after getting elected, they are going to get short shrift if the request for a reset isn't underpinned by action on the UK side. And the UK is not without cards to play in those future negotiations – the EU could be tempted with deals on fish quotas; easier mobility for its professionals, students and young people; better cooperation on EU–UK energy transfers; and a deeper relationship on science and research – an area where the UK is in many respects out in front of the EU. Such alignment would also make it easier to manage the Irish Sea border under the Windsor Framework and reduce flashpoints between Westminster, Edinburgh and Cardiff.

As was demonstrated by the 2023 negotiation over Northern Ireland, with the right approach, common sense can prevail. The rancour of the 2017–19 negotiation does not have to be repeated. That clash often descended into a zero-sum game, partly because the EU was determined to make it into a pedagogical exercise on the perils of leaving the bloc. Well, mission accomplished. As one EU official put it, the Brexit negotiations served as a 'useful booster shot' for the EU single market, creating long-lasting antibodies among EU member states against future attempts to undermine the 'four freedoms'. But by 2026 it will be nearly a decade since the Brexit referendum. The EU and the UK may now be divided, but they sit together in the shadow of looming global crises on climate, the fallout from the Ukraine war and the threat of an increasingly nationalist and assertive China. It must be worth trying to forge a more consensual, common approach this time around, that brings us much closer to the associate relationship to which the EU and the UK must ultimately aspire. The disastrous alternative is that a decade of EU–UK estrangement is allowed to settle into a permanent state of affairs.

13

Fixing What Can Be Fixed

Although the EU–UK Trade and Cooperation Agreement is a deeply limited document when compared to full membership of the single market, it is a starting point. As Peter Mandelson put it, the TCA should be viewed as 'a ground floor and not a ceiling' to the UK's future relationships with the EU. On the positive side, the governing Partnership Council which sits atop the TCA's 32 operational committees and working groups has quite broad powers to amend and improve the deal without seeking a fresh mandate from the 27 member states of the European Council. In key areas like the 'rules of origin' or the rights of EU and UK professionals to work in each other's countries, the text says the Council can agree to amendments and 'possible improvements in their mutual interest'.

Of course, the operative word there is 'mutual'. A new UK government might argue there is a common interest in improving the rights of each other's architects or tour guides to work in the EU, the European Commission might even agree, but to win that concession it will need to convince national lobby groups. French tour operators might be perfectly happy to see work that was previously done by British professional service operators being snapped up by local providers. Any request to improve the TCA will also have to overcome the fact that Brussels will always be wary that any concessions granted to the UK might then be demanded from other albeit smaller countries on the EU periphery like Switzerland, Turkey, Norway or Ukraine. Over time the UK, acting as a strategic partner with the EU, could argue its case to be treated differently from these smaller countries, but the framing of that conversation would need to be fundamentally different than in the last seven years.

The UK will also have to be patient. Trade talks quickly become both technical and often adversarial, leading to long, grinding negotiations with often quite limited outcomes. For example, the EU–Canada trade deal, CETA, also contained scope to 'mutually recognise' each other's professional qualifications, but since that deal was signed in 2016 the two sides had only managed a single side-deal – on architects – by the end of 2022. And that took nine rounds of negotiations that were spread over nearly a year. Since Brexit, the British public may have come to expect the drama of EU–UK 'tunnels' and crunch, eleventh-hour negotiations, but these were driven by the threat of mutually destructive 'no-deal' outcomes or the risk of further destabilisation of the political environment in Northern Ireland. In those circumstances the EU and the UK had a mutual interest in cutting a deal. Now, with TCA and the Windsor Framework on Northern Ireland in place, the same negotiating dynamics do not apply.

This much has already become clear from the tenor of EU-UK interactions since the Windsor framework came into force, with the European Commission making it clear that on a host of issues – from joining the Horizon science programs, electric vehicle tariffs, repatriating euro clearing to the EU and financial services co-operation – there will be no special treatment for the UK. As European Commission officials are at pains to point out, the deal on Northern Ireland may have got the UK out of the diplomatic deep freeze but it doesn't change the fact that the UK remains a so-called 'third country'. As one senior EU official put it: 'The UK should not expect any special treatment because it has belatedly agreed to implement the Protocol on Northern Ireland – with generous concessions – which was the deal the UK had anyway signed up to itself three years ago.' So while UK institutions advance ideas to bring the EU-UK relationship closer, the UK government should be under no illusions about just how hard it will be to shift the dial on a trade deal which, in many respects, suits the EU. It will take serious and focused diplomatic effort combined with a rethink over current red lines. Because as Stefan Fuehring, the lead European Commission official overseeing the TCA, warned at the EU-UK Forum annual conference in

June 2023, the UK should not confuse its own desires to improve the TCA with the EU's. 'There's almost on a bi-weekly basis a report [on how to improve the existing Brexit deal] coming from the Tony Blair Institute, the UK in a Changing Europe, the House of Lords and so on. My job is to follow all these, of course, but I'm not aware that in the last two years any such report has come out of the EU system,' he said. 'We have really moved on now with this debate [over Brexit] and I think the next decade is one where we'll deal with future member states, rather than a past member state.'

And even if the UK can bring about a more fundamental reset, as the CBI business group observed in its plan to address some of the deficiencies in the deal, 'building significant levels of ambition on the TCA will be a marathon, not a sprint'. But all journeys, however long, must begin somewhere. Even before the TCA comes up for formal five-year review the UK can start to make better use of the deal, now that the Windsor Framework has unblocked the EU–UK political relationship. At the mundane level, for example, the TCA included provision for a 'Working Group on Motor Vehicles and Parts' to help with industry co-ordination, but during the stand-off over Northern Ireland industry associations report it was never convened. Such meetings are just the baby steps. How far the UK can ultimately travel down that road will depend on politics on both sides of the Channel, but there are a host of areas where the business community would like to see the deal deepened – many will require bartering with the EU, but not all. There are also some long overdue steps that the UK can take unilaterally to improve the operating environment for UK businesses. Here are some of the options and areas the negotiators will need to consider.

The Nitty-gritty

SPS Deal and Veterinary Agreement

One of the biggest hurdles to trade at any external EU border are checks and paperwork related to sanitary and phytosanitary (SPS) controls, which are there to protect animal, plant or public health. The rules are immensely complex, requiring exporters to fill in forms with hundreds of lines and get them signed off by a vet. That's not a massive problem if you're sending a whole container of frozen lamb from New Zealand, or a single consignment of chicken ready-meals from Thailand, which can take weeks to arrive by container ship. But for the high-frequency roll-on, roll-off trade border between Dover and Calais, where single trucks can carry hundreds of different product lines, it creates a bureaucratic minefield. The result is that two years after the Brexit trade deal came into force, UK food and drink exports to the EU were still smaller than they were in 2019, and yet food exports to non-EU countries had grown by more than 17 per cent over the same period.

The obvious fix is for the UK to negotiate an agreement with the EU to either align completely with the EU's rules on SPS, or failing that, reach an agreement where the EU recognises that UK standards are essentially equivalent. This would eliminate or significantly reduce checks at the border, smoothing trade flows in agrifood products and help the food exports to the EU start to grow again. It could also put live products like British mussels and other molluscs back on Continental menus after they were banned because of Brexit. Trade groups, including the CBI and the Food and Drink Federation, have repeatedly called for such a deal to support an industry which is the UK's largest manufacturing sector, employing nearly 500,000 people and contributing almost £30 billion to the UK economy.

Successive post-Brexit Conservative governments have ignored these demands, while the Labour Party has committed to such a deal. The European Commission offered the UK a Swiss-style veterinary agreement as part of attempts to help reduce the Irish Sea border thrown up by the Northern Ireland Protocol, but even so an SPS agreement will take some negotiating. The EU may feel in a position to demand the UK 'dynamically' aligns with the EU, automatically following new EU rules. That would be a problem for some UK producers who might baulk at accepting stringent new standards on the use of pesticides used to protect crops of oats and oilseed rape. As ever, there are trade-offs. One immediate step the UK could take to level the playing field in any negotiation would be to start to impose long-delayed border checks on EU food exports to the UK. That might make it tougher for UK supermarkets to keep their shelves stocked, but it would create a mutual incentive for the European Commission to strike a deal to reduce SPS frictions at the UK border for its exporters.

The obvious downside for the UK from an EU–UK SPS agreement, whether dynamic or based on equivalence, is that it is highly incompatible with Brexiters' dreams of negotiating a comprehensive FTA with the United States. Such a deal has been talismanic for Brexiters even though, by the government's own estimates, it would increase UK GDP by only 0.07 per cent in the long-run. US negotiators have also made it clear that a deal would require the UK to accept US food products made to non-EU standards, raising the prospect of the UK allowing imports of chlorine-washed chicken and other food imports that do not comply with EU standards. This would then massively re-complicate UK food exports to the EU. But since only 13 per cent of UK food and drink exports by value went to the US in 2022 – compared with nearly 60 per cent to the EU – it surely makes sense to prioritise friction-free exports to Europe rather than America where UK food exports have in any case grown strongly in recent years, despite not having an FTA.

Visas and Mobility

Among the biggest practical gripes about Brexit is the difficulty of moving around the EU, whether for young people looking to brush up their English by getting a summer bar job in London, or businesses waiting weeks for permits to relocate staff between offices in the UK and Europe. Such, of course, is life outside the EU single market and, in the spirit of 'no cherry-picking', Brussels will always be quick to remind Brits that there cannot be a facsimile of free movement, where the UK gets many of the rights that come with EU membership without accepting the obligations, like budget contributions and oversight from the European Court of Justice.

But within those parameters there are still improvements that the UK could look to make, including in some areas that will be attractive to the EU, like visas that would grant easier access for European students attending UK universities. After Brexit the UK quit the EU's Erasmus student exchange programme causing a sharp fall in the number of EU students attending UK universities. That's because EU students now either have to use a standard visitor visa route, which is valid only for six months (no use if you're on a year-long language placement) or spend hundreds of pounds on a short-term study visa or a full student visa, including a £470 surcharge to cover NHS treatment.

A different government with a more flexible attitude to immigration could change this offer, and lower the cost of the one-year visa, scrapping the surcharge in favour of proof of health insurance, as with the EU's much cheaper Student Schengen Visa. The UK, unlike many EU countries, also has no Internship Visa for young people to take training and work placements – this makes it hard for UK colleges and businesses to enter into reciprocal exchange programmes. The UK higher education industry would support these moves. Both UK and EU universities are desperate that links that abounded before Brexit shouldn't wither on the vine. And as with trade, the longer such barriers to entry persist the more relationships will wither and the harder it will be to restore them. EU universities will simply forge other links with colleges in Canada, the US or Singapore, and the UK will be the loser.

Education is just one area where, in the right political environment, there is a clear mutual interest in the EU and the UK making agreements that facilitate exchange. Musicians and other performers, as we have seen, is another. In the case of school trips, the UK government could reinstate something like the group visas on which parties of schoolchildren happily travelled before Brexit. More broadly, an EU-wide Youth Mobility Scheme for 18–30-year-olds would also be a massive boost to the outbound travel industry (in both directions) but more importantly help to underwrite the well-being of EU–UK relations for future generations. The UK already has such an arrangement with other countries, including Japan and Canada, which grants visas to live and work up to two years in the UK as long as you can demonstrate you have savings of £2,500. The EU has a similar scheme with its own trade deal with Canada. The EU will not accept discrimination between different member states and is likely to resist limits or quotas on such a scheme, but since Youth Mobility Schemes do not provide a route to residency or setting up a business, politicians should sell such a deal unapologetically as a mutual good, and face down any suggestion that it amounts to a 'return to free movement via the backdoor'. The EU and UK tourism industries would also find mutual benefit in a specific, reciprocal agreement to enable coach drivers to remain for more than 90 days in any 180-day period.

Lastly, businesses on both sides also want to see improvements for moving staff back and forth across the Channel – so-called 'intra-company transferees'. This has become time-consuming and expensive since Brexit, with the CBI warning that visa processing times have a 'potential knock-on impact on supply chains and damage to the business model'. Although these issues are caused by individual countries' visa bureaucracies, there is a strong mutual interest in an EU-wide agreement to speed up and standardise the process. An EU visa that allowed 180 days in any 365-day period – rather than 90 days in every 180, which is the rule for countries of the Schengen free movement zone – would also help seasonal workers.

Linking EU and UK Carbon Pricing Schemes

This eventuality has already been foreseen in the deal. The existing TCA text says that the EU and the UK will give 'serious consideration' to linking their respective carbon-pricing systems. With the EU actively planning to introduce a new carbon border adjustment tax, UK industry fears that unless the UK aligns with the EU's framework then UK exporters will face a massive bureaucratic headache, providing certificates attesting to the carbon emissions associated with individual consignments of imported steel, for example. There will be arguments from some quarters that the UK should not be a 'rule-taker' when it comes to net zero and that an independent UK carbon-pricing and CBAM scheme will allow the UK to build a bespoke policy framework specifically to meet the UK's net zero 2050 goal. The question will be whether those benefits outweigh the costs imposed by needing to reduce frictions on access to the EU market.

VAT Improvements

The Trade and Cooperation Agreement contains repeated commitments to make trade as easy as possible for small and medium-sized enterprises, but as we have seen for many smaller companies, trading with the EU has become a bureaucratic nightmare. Top of the list of many such companies' difficulties is handling VAT on sales to the EU, according to surveys by the British Chambers of Commerce, with different EU countries having differing approaches to VAT collection on imports. Companies making smaller sales of under €150 via the EU's Import One-Stop Shop (IOSS) for goods have to appoint an EU 'fiscal representative' (a registered company able to declare and pay VAT) to complete the transaction.

With EU VAT rules expected to continue to evolve and diverge further from the UK's, the British Chambers of Commerce (BCC) would like the UK to try to negotiate easier arrangements, including an agreement similar to that enjoyed by Norway, which limits the requirement to have a fiscal intermediary in the EU. Given the scale of the issues caused by VAT, the BCC has suggested that a future government should look at the cost–benefit analysis of returning to a common VAT framework between the UK and the EU. This would remove the UK's flexibility to zero-rate some products. This became a talismanic issue during the Brexit debate when it came to female sanitary products – what Brexit campaigners called the EU's 'tampon tax' – although the EU has since changed its rules on this to allow selective zero-rating on these.

Rules of Origin

As we have seen with the car industry, the TCA has quite restrictive 'rules of origin'. These do not allow UK companies to count inputs from other EU FTA partners as 'UK originating content' when calculating if their product is sufficiently 'made in the UK' to get zero-tariff access to the EU single market. The TCA does enable the Partnership Council to amend the terms of the 'rules of origin' by mutual agreement, but given that the 27-member single market makes it easier for EU companies to have products 50 per cent 'made in EU', it is not clear why the EU would shift from the deal made in 2020. But where there is a mutual interest – for example if, as anticipated, the EU car industry is not able to make 'rules of origin' targets for cars by 1 January 2024 – it would make sense to negotiate temporary flexibilities. Otherwise the EU and the UK will be imposing a 10 per cent tariff on electric vehicles, which makes no sense when both the EU and UK are trying to encourage motorists to go electric. Longer term, if the EU continues to win the race to build EV gigafactories, it may see strategic self-interest in continuing to squeeze the UK

The British Chambers of Commerce has also suggested that the UK seriously considers joining the Pan-Euro-Mediterranean Convention (PEM) which is an agreement between the EU and a group of 20 countries, including Norway, Switzerland, Turkey and Israel, to have common rules of origin. The UK needs to conduct a detailed cost–benefit analysis for different industries. The longer this takes, the less value there may be in joining the PEM as impacted companies move their supply chains away from the EU. Joining the PEM would help broaden the supply chain network for some UK exporters, particularly in the apparel and textile industry, but would be complicated by the fact that the rules of origin in the TCA aren't compatible with those of the PEM. Either the TCA rules of origin need to be replaced by those of the PEM. Or potentially it may be possible to operate two systems in parallel, but that would be subject to negotiation with the EU and require Brussels to agree to exceptional treatment for the UK.

Conformity Assessment

During the 2020 negotiations the UK tried to get a deal from Brussels that would enable products to be certified in the UK as conforming to EU standards. The EU has agreed deals on so-called 'mutual recognition of conformity assessment' bodies with other FTA partners, including Australia, Canada, Japan, New Zealand, the USA, Israel and Switzerland, so could in theory do the same for the UK. During the 2020 negotiations Michel Barnier set out the rationale for not giving a similar deal to the UK, saying Brussels was not going to enable Britain to become a 'certification hub' off the coast of Europe. That was another expression of Brussels' determination that the UK should not benefit from quitting the EU or achieve even a faint facsimile of single market benefits, but seven years after the Brexit vote, the EU might feel rather less threatened. Whether that position might shift, particularly in a world where the British government was pledging to align more deeply on EU regulations across a wide range of areas, would be an important question for the negotiations.

The UK government should also end the 'vanity exercise' of having a UKCA mark where it is just duplicating the EU's CE mark, causing pain for businesses who have to have dual sets of label and expensive duplicate testing of products. In areas where the UK accepts the same underlying standards as the EU, the British Chambers of Commerce has argued that the government should permanently recognise the CE mark in the UK. The UK government has already announced that from 2024 its medical devices regulator, the Medicines and Healthcare products Regulatory Agency (MHRA) will grant 'automatic sign-off' for medicines and technologies already approved by other trusted regulators around the globe such as in the US, EU and Japan.

UK REACH

As we have seen, duplicating the EU's 'Registration, Evaluation, Authorisation and Restriction of Chemicals' or REACH safety regime in the UK is costing the industry billions of pounds, reducing the range of new chemicals being put on the market in the UK and damaging the prospects of UK companies with their EU clients. The UK regulator, the Health and Safety Executive, which is still consulting on how to operate the UK's copycat version of REACH in 2023, needs to urgently deliver clarity for the industry on how a light-touch registration regime should work for existing chemicals. The UK could consider whether to create a simple notification scheme that would recognise that chemicals that have registered with EU REACH are valid for use in the UK.

This would ease burdens on business, but is not without complications. Without a bespoke data-sharing agreement with the European Chemicals Agency (ECHA) the UK regulator will be partially sighted and unable to access the non-public data elements on which ECHA registrations are based. The UK would be electing to systematically hang its entire regulatory system off data held in another jurisdiction. The UK and EU chemicals industries lobbied for a data-sharing agreement during the 2020 negotiations but it never materialised. The UK could also seek to negotiate a deeper agreement to allow the respective regulators to cooperate better and share information on chemicals of concern. Similar memorandums of understanding exist between the EU with Canada and Australia, but this would not address the fundamental issue with REACH, which is that the UK doesn't have access to the underlying commercial data that validates safety registrations.

Recognising Professional Qualifications

By the standards of free trade deals, the TCA contains quite expansive provisions on services, but these still do little to facilitate services trade between the EU and the UK. The provisions that are in the deal are sector-by-sector and via individual EU member states, which leaves UK services access far short of that enjoyed under single market membership. The deal has a chapter on legal services, but beyond that, there is no broad provision for professionals to provide their services freely in the EU. Business people can make short-term visits to the EU (a maximum of 90 days in a six-month period) to scope out opportunities, but they are not automatically allowed to sell goods or provide services to the public or fulfil contracts for other businesses. The EU and the UK also no longer automatically recognise each other's professional qualifications, and the TCA contains an exhaustive list of the restrictions that each EU country places on each UK profession to operate in the EU. As noted above with Canada's efforts to get a deal on architects, these can be expanded by mutual agreement, and the Partnership Council has powers to 'review, develop and adopt' new arrangements for professional qualifications if they can be mutually agreed. It may well take time and effort, as well as concerted lobbying from business interests inside the EU, but there is potential scope to improve the ability of UK professionals to practise in the EU, and vice-versa. This, allied with a lighter-touch regime for intra-company transferees, would be of value to some service providers.

Unlocking the Lugano Convention

Before Brexit the UK was part of the Lugano Convention, an important treaty which handles international legal disputes. The

UK asked to rejoin the Convention in April 2020 as an individual member, but its accession required the consent of all members, including the European Commission. During the long-running row over the Northern Ireland Protocol the Commission blocked the UK's request to rejoin, to the annoyance of London law firms. The resolution of the Northern Ireland dispute should in theory unlock the UK re-accession to Lugano, although some EU member states may be content to let the UK sweat as long as possible in order to weaken the attraction of the British capital as a centre for international dispute resolution.

Customs Symmetry – Better Cooperation and Enforcement

A more productive atmosphere between the EU and the UK could also lead to some streamlining of customs procedures between the EU and the UK. As mentioned above, the UK introducing equivalent border controls to the EU after years of delays might concentrate minds in Brussels about the need to reduce frictions.

There is no wishing away customs formalities, but both the UK and the EU are in the process of developing a so-called 'single trade window' which will digitally combine the multiple strands of paperwork needed to trade across borders. These schemes will come into force from 2025 (with a pretty basic version) and will take more than a decade to implement. Trade specialists are clear these new computer systems will not be a magic bullet for trade frictions, and are urging the UK and EU to cooperate over system specification to ensure that they are as interoperable as possible.

Better relations at EU level might also help to address the frustrations felt by British exporters when different EU countries interpret EU rules on food products or organic standards differently. That was one reason why Kiran Tawadey of Hampstead Tea decided to set up a distribution warehouse in the Netherlands, because customs authorities in Germany, Italy and France were all taking different interpretations of rules on organic certifications. Such is life outside the EU single market, but Brussels would no doubt complain if British ports started demanding different documents for the same products. The UK could justifiably push for more consistency from the EU.

The UK could also apply to join the EU/EEA's Safety and Security Zone which would eliminate the need for hauliers to lodge pre-notifications when importing and exporting. These documents can run to 30 or 40 data fields, creating unnecessary expense. During the 2020 trade negotiation the UK decided not to seek a waiver on security declaration, sparking fury from the shipping and haulage industries, which accused the government of putting 'political dogma above the economic well-being of the country'. Trade specialists say that with a different political approach, this decision could easily be reversed.

The UK could also do more to help itself. British trade associations like the CBI, the British Chambers of Commerce and the Food and Drink Federation have repeatedly called for a better one-stop-shop trade portal for UK exporters. Using the guidance on exporting on gov.uk websites is frequently 'time-consuming and not fruitful' according to a CBI survey of members. Traders complain that gov.uk takes them in frustrating loops that do not provide usable information that they need to export. As it is, most companies simply don't have the expertise or the bandwidth to comb through the texts of trade deals to find out the rules of origin for individual products. They need easy access to ready-to-use information to help them get their products on the way. The government could do a much, much better job of providing this.

14

Fighting for a Better Future

The hard truth remains, however, that even quite substantial upgrades to the EU–UK Trade and Cooperation Agreement will have limited overall economic impact. For as long as current political red lines rule out membership of a customs union with the EU and the EU single market, the UK will remain structurally disadvantaged. Some sectors, like the food and drink industry, will benefit significantly from an improved trade deal with the EU, but overall the UK will see a steady erosion of competitiveness when it comes to trading with Europe. Which is why the UK's response to its Brexit predicament cannot be limited solely to trying to partially stitch back together what was broken by Brexit. Any moves to patch the Brexit-inflicted slow-puncture in the UK economy are to be welcomed, but that must not conceal the scale of the UK's post-Brexit challenge.

If the UK's political leaders are convinced that the acceptable price of Brexit freedom is an economy that is 3 to 5 per cent smaller – which is the central range of forecasts – then the imperative to generate economic growth becomes all the stronger. That means confronting painful domestic reforms – on education, land use and tax – while developing growth strategies that outlast five-year election cycles. Post-Brexit Britain, quite literally, cannot afford more of the wishful thinking that has blighted UK policy-making since the 2016 referendum. That is the argument for political leadership that dares to confront the Brexit bind in which the UK now finds itself, rather pretending that not talking about Brexit will make it all go away.

It is difficult to be optimistic, given the last seven years, but that post-Brexit reckoning needs to take place with urgency and honesty. Anaesthetising the debate around the consequences of

Brexit will lead to political torpor, not an energetic debate about how the UK can find a new place in the world. Jeremy Hunt's soothing tones that the UK, over time, will replicate the benefits of single market membership is misleading; more importantly, it underplays the deep-seated productivity challenges the UK economy now faces. These were evident before Brexit, but after leaving the EU the UK now faces additional headwinds as it tries to plot a course to a more prosperous future. It is sobering to reflect that the UK is now, on average, 21 per cent poorer than Australia, Canada, France, Germany, and the Netherlands, according to the Resolution Foundation – countries that the UK would have long considered to be its peers. On the 'glass-half-full' approach to life, however, that does at least provide plenty of room for improvement. No one lives the counter-factual life, but on current growth trends, GDP per head in Poland will outstrip the UK's by the end of the decade, according to World Bank data. The message from the next government, therefore, needs to be not 'steady as she goes', but 'all hands on deck' to create an investment climate that is attractive to the world, notwithstanding the UK's self-marginalisation in Europe.

Much of this work must begin at home. The UK can move to repair its diplomatic relations with Brussels and EU capitals; it can try to smooth down some of the rough edges of the TCA, but that is just the bare minimum needed to get Britain back on track. Brexiters argued that leaving the EU and 'taking back control' would ultimately deliver a better Britain because outside the EU the UK had nowhere to hide. Britain's destiny, they said, was now in British hands. Or as Dominic Cummings put it: 'The EU has narrowed our horizons. It has narrowed everyone's horizons in Whitehall so they're not thinking about the big things in the world. They're not thinking about the forces changing it or what Britain can really do to contribute to them.' Those are fine words, but seven years after Brexit it's clear that the shock-therapy of leaving the EU hasn't revitalised Britain, it's just laid us low.

The incoherence of Brexit has manifested itself in self-defeating policies at home that have diminished the UK's standing in the world and reduced its attractiveness to investors. As Paul Nurse wrote in his Independent Review into the UK's research and innovation landscape, for example, the failure to secure access to the EU's Horizon science programme 'has damaged the UK's standing' and made it harder to recruit 'international talent'. Similarly, the now-abandoned madcap pledge to expunge all EU-derived law from the UK statute book in a single year (laws on which vast swathes of British economic and social life were based for 40 years) served as an international advertisement for Britain's Brexit funk. The frustrating part is that while only a tiny minority of ideological Brexiters thought a bonfire of EU-derived law was a good idea, the vast majority of people agreed that there were areas where the UK could profitably regulate differently from the EU. But rather than seek to capitalise on that point of agreement, successive post-Brexit governments have preferred to allow the Bill to become a source of division and instability.

As a result, Brexit, far from unleashing Britain's creative potential, has just created regulatory uncertainty and additional barriers to trade. If the search for a Brexit deregulatory dividend was easy or straightforward then, seven years after Brexit, a clear path to regulatory upsides would have surely emerged. It has not. It's time to think again. Because regulation is a double-edged sword, both stabilising and stultifying – it can be an enabling force for business, as well as a source of cost and irritation. As the CBI business lobby has repeated *ad nauseam*, downsides need to be weighed carefully against any potential upsides. This is about delivery, not ideology.

What is now required is a targeted and proportional approach that listens to industry, not the musings of 'weirdos and misfits'. The regulation of the future economy, in industries like AI, gene editing or the Internet of Things, is increasingly global. Everyone else is innovating and regulating too. There's a reason why the EU's primal fear that a deregulating, 'go-it-alone' Britain could out-compete Europe hasn't been borne out. Because as the UK in a Changing Europe's divergence tracker shows, in the vast majority of areas regulatory gravity has taken over. The UK hasn't gone anywhere because in a great majority of cases it's not practical or advantageous to do so. This is because, as the head of the CBI said in a landmark speech in early 2023, 'divergence is high-stake politics and economics' and the UK cannot avoid the EU's counterplays. A dogmatic commitment to divergence from the EU has swaddled British business in red tape. As the CBI observed, it is a bitter irony that, 'the party of deregulation risks simply doubling the amount we have'.

So it is time to get past the simplistic anti-EU approach to

Brexit that has clouded the UK's collective judgement since 2016. The UK can commit to close alignment with the EU in legacy industries like cars and chemicals while looking to innovate in future industries. Where it does so, it can look to lead by example and collaborate with other global regulators. Now the UK is outside the EU, stability, transparency and credibility are even more important than during EU membership. It may have been sclerotic and frustrating, but EU regulation was nothing if not predictable. After Brexit, the UK, by definition, is in a perpetual position of uncertainty since the EU's regulatory frameworks are constantly evolving, even when the UK stands still. That is why building a reliable, deliberative framework that consults business is essential to generating investor confidence. The suggestion by the independent UK Trade and Business Commission to set up an EU-UK 'Regulatory Cooperation Council' so London and Brussels can coordinate on regulation, as well as a new 'Board of Trade' to serve as an independent watchdog performing cost-benefit analysis for UK trade policy, are both worth considering.

As the CBI argued, better and bespoke regulation can pay dividends – the UK has demonstrated just that in the past with the global success of the City of London – but first 'you have to run the numbers to make sure it's not a complete own goal'. Take a recent example of post-Brexit success: in 2015 the UK financial regulator the Financial Conduct Authority (FCA) set up the world's first regulatory 'sandbox' to create a controlled space for fintech companies to experiment with new products. The system helped propel the UK to the top of the league in Europe for fintech, with the UK boasting thirty-two billion-dollar companies, or 'unicorns', by mid-2022 – four times as many as France and the Netherlands, which were the EU countries with the next largest number. This is an example of how the UK can set the standard by pioneering open data for finance, making new business models possible – a lead which the EU is now following with its own similar reforms.

But the EU is also not standing still in other areas. In 2023 the European Commission announced regulatory sandboxes for using blockchain outside the financial services sector and in some key areas of environment and technology – online safety, cyber resilience and single-use plastics – has actually regulated faster than the UK since Brexit. There are other future industries where the UK is well-placed to prosper – agritech, gene editing, AI, quantum – but the UK will not succeed in isolation and by antagonising the EU. As Paul Nurse advised, a go-it-alone approach will not work given that the EU is one of the world's three major science communities, alongside the US and China. On the contrary, 'relationships with European collaborators need to be protected, maintained and expanded, so that the free exchange of researchers, ideas and data established in recent years, which are all vital to UK RDI, is not damaged'.

The UK must also get better at delivery. Rhetorical ambition about the future too often is not matched by reality. There are some areas where independence from EU regulatory frameworks could allow the UK to play the role of 'incubator' for future technologies – for example in the lucrative business of conducting clinical trials for new drugs and therapies. A single drug trial can bring in £400 million, deliver therapeutic benefits to NHS patients and create high-quality jobs for UK scientists, data specialists and trial managers. But as things stand, the UK lags behind Belgium and Spain in terms of ease of clinical trial management, according to John Bell, who helped develop the AstraZeneca Covid-19 vaccine and has contributed to the Sunak government's innovation reform agenda.

In an industry where speed-to-market is all-important, Bell believes the UK could steal a march on those two EU market leaders if its regulator was nimbler than the ponderous European Medicines Agency (EMA), which regulates on behalf of 27 countries. But to win the race, says Bell, the UK has to put its own house in order and make better use of the unique data trove generated by the NHS. This isn't first and foremost about undercutting the EU, it's about fixing things at home. For example, an approval from the NHS's parsimonious drugs watchdog NICE is highly valued by global companies because it demonstrates the cost-saving properties of their product – unfortunately, it currently takes up to 300 days to obtain. That's just far too long, says Bell.

British governments talking endlessly about hypothetical opportunities in future tech is not the same as them actually delivering on these ambitions. And the UK's track record of delivery is often dispiritingly poor for many of the same reasons – bureaucratic sclerosis and an overbearing centralised bureaucracy – for which Brexiters love to criticise the EU. Clinical trials are indeed a good potential post-Brexit opportunity for the UK, but the number of UK trials actually fell by 41 per cent between 2017 and 2021. This despite repeated Whitehall reviews to fix the problem. Yet another review was announced in February 2023 that, the government said, was 'building on' the existing 'ten-year vision' for clinical trials, that was published in March 2021, just two years previously. In short, talking isn't the same as doing. 'Everything is about execution,' says Bell, who contributed to Patrick Vallance's review into pro-growth innovation. 'The UK has opportunities but we just have to get better at delivery because the reality is we have just not been very good at it.'

Ultimately, Brexit has created barriers to trade, but that doesn't necessarily have to mean – to use a word that has been on the lips of many UK CEOs over the last five years – that the UK is 'uninvestable'. The UK has much to offer compared to EU competitors – less onerous labour relations than France, less bureaucracy than Italy, stronger rule of law than Hungary. There are myriad reasons to invest in the UK over those countries, but Brexit has undoubtedly made it harder – and having created this frictional disadvantage, the UK will have to work smarter to get on. That could, as Cummings suggested, be a transformative, invigorating process – everyone should want the Brexiters to be proved right that the UK can be better off outside the EU – but that will only happen if the ultimate fallout from Brexit is that it forces the UK to confront the reasons why it is sliding down global economic league tables.

Mindless boosterism is no substitute for a coherent industrial strategy that looks to translate the UK's undoubted scientific prowess into higher productivity and wages. Brexiter ministers never tire of citing the fact that the UK has four of the world's top ten universities (and that the EU has none) but that does not, in and of itself, mean the UK is a 'scientific superpower' or an 'innovation nation'. As things stand, it isn't. When it comes to productive R&D the UK is brilliant at research, but very much less good at development. Despite a government pledge to boost UK research investment after decades of underperformance, the UK still lags other advanced economies by significant margins. In 2022 the UK spent 2.7 per cent of GDP on R&D – still far behind the USA, South Korea and Germany, which invested between 3.2 per cent and 4.6 per cent. When it comes to UK government expenditure on R&D, the UK was ranked 27th out of 36 advanced OECD nations. As the Nurse review bluntly put it: 'The UK Government's present level of R&D funding will be inadequate to drive the economic and societal benefits that the Government desires.'

Put another way, for as long as current political red lines on the single market and customs union persist, 'fixing Brexit' won't, first and foremost, be about Brexit. It will be about putting the UK's own house in order. A government less desperate to justify Brexit will be freer to frame these reforms in a forward-looking way. The government's Edinburgh Reforms of the financial services sector were touted as an example of 'Brexit opportunities', but as the Tory chair of the Treasury select committee Harriet Baldwin pointed out, only 18 of the 30 proposals had anything to do with leaving the EU. And those that did, like the reforms of the Solvency II regulations designed to release up to £100 billion of investment capital from insurance and pension funds, have been a long time coming. So long, in fact, that very similar EU reforms may happen first.

The hope is that releasing UK pension fund capital will reduce the number of British start-ups being sucked out of the UK to the US where there is a much deeper pool of capital and managerial talent needed to scale up companies. The UK has shown itself it is good at building innovative companies; the still unanswered question is whether it can build future industries. Regulatory divergence from the EU is only one small piece of that puzzle. Success will also require inculcating a new culture of ambition and risk-taking in Britain alongside a laundry list of structural fixes like housing and planning reforms; narrowing the gap between state and private education, and upgrading UK workplace skills; re-densifying our cities and creating stronger city-clusters while sticking to the liberal immigration policy that attracts the best talent in the world. All that requires strong governance and patient frontline delivery – not a moonshot mentality or magical thinking.

Because while there has been no shortage of strategy documents and reviews raining down from Whitehall since Brexit, these have the opposite effect than intended when so many go unimplemented. Economic red herrings like freeports, or projects like Liz Truss's mayfly 'investment zones' have become symbols of the UK's restless and fretful governance that deters investment. Much of this is a direct function of leaving the EU. Programmes like Horizon, Erasmus and EU regional development funds were bureaucratic to administer, but they ran on predictable, seven-year cycles that allowed for long-term planning and investment. Since Brexit, these have been replaced by scattergun schemes like the Levelling Up Fund, the Communities Fund, or the Shared Prosperity Fund that have been just as bureaucratic as the EU predecessors, only with added Whitehall chaos. The result has been atomised pots of funding delivered at local-council level on an annual basis with little obvious strategic planning, other than to give MPs something to put on their leaflets at election time. As Paul Nurse observed in his innovation landscape review, research organisations, investors, global companies and researchers 'all have concerns about short-term decision-making', warning that it undermined the confidence needed to 'operate, interact and invest' in the UK. Identical criticisms could be levelled at other key strategic policy areas – like achieving net zero, developing innovation and skills, healthcare and well-being – that all require thinking that goes beyond the reactive, pinball policy-making of the post-Brexit era.

Ultimately, the opportunity cost of Brexit is that it has proved a colossal distraction at a critical juncture. What is now needed is a realistic, sober vision for what Britain should look like in 2050 – allied to fact-based strategies for how to get there, along with a determination to deliver where previously we have failed. There is no time to lose, because for the last seven years the UK got lost 'playing chicken with itself', and while we were absorbed in our private family squabble, the rest of the world was quietly moving on, building gigafactories and new strategic alliances to which the UK is not party. As a midsize power with undoubted soft-power credentials, the UK can thrive as a global convenor of talent and enterprise, but only by building on international relationships of trust. Those relationships have been damaged by Brexit, and they will need to be restored, but a political space is now emerging at home and abroad for that process to begin. There can be no escaping that Brexit leaves Britain in a bind, but as the UK slips further behind peer economies that also creates a burning platform. In the best sense of the word, the UK now needs to come out fighting.

Acknowledgements

The privilege of being a reporter is that you have *carte blanche* to ask questions. There is no shame in asking experts for basic explanations of complex issues; the journalist's job is to render those explanations intelligible and interesting for a general reader. That is why, above all else, this is a reporter's book. It leans heavily on the expertise and experience of a large collection of professors, lawyers, business executives, civil servants and trade experts who, over the last seven years, have helped me to trace the evolution of Brexit from campaign trail concept to concrete reality. Wherever possible, I've acknowledged those experts directly in the body of the text. If at any point I have inadvertently garbled their work despite my best endeavours, the fault is mine, not theirs.

Because this is a journalistic rather than academic book, it is deliberately not weighed down by footnotes and other paraphernalia. With one or two tiny exceptions where anonymity is required to protect the identity of those who are not licensed to speak to journalists, I have deliberately tried to limit myself to quoting exclusively from the public record – politicians' speeches, select committee transcripts, archive interviews, think-tank reports, newspaper articles, academic papers and trade groups' policy documents and surveys – all of which are easily findable via an internet search. This is not, therefore, an accounting of Brexit that relies on insider information. The UK's Brexit journey is there in plain sight, for anyone who cares to go looking for it.

Aside from the many people I interviewed to gather ideas for this book, there are, however, some people who went far above and beyond the call of duty, taking time out of busy lives to read early drafts. This helped immensely to catch mistakes and smooth over rough edges. For this, special thanks to: Michael Gasiorek, Charles Grant, Sophie Hale, Ned Hawes, Steve Hawes, Katy Hayward, David Henig, Peter Holmes, Anna Jerzewska, Patrick Keating, Sam Lowe, Adam Marshall, Andrew McCormick, Anand Menon, Mark Mistry, Jonathan Portes, George Riddell, Anton Spisak and John Springford.

Any book is a collaborative effort between author and publisher, but this one would never have been written without the prompting of Jenny Fry and Simon Thorogood at Canongate, where the team has worked furiously to produce the manuscript under considerable time pressure. Thanks to Daniel Garrahan for making the film that planted the seed and to Lucy Warwick-Ching for playing matchmaker. Books also take time to write and I'm grateful to *Financial Times* editor Roula Khalaf and ever-generous *FT* colleagues for allowing me the space to get it done. Thanks to Chris Cook for playing backstop; and Andrew Parker and Siona Jenkins for taking the day-to-day strain in my absence.

Lastly, none of this is possible without the patience and support of my family. Book writing is a solitary business that brings with it a certain amount of sleepless nights as my wife, Clare, knows better than anyone. So for all those evenings and weekends when I was distracted at the dinner table, only half-present when I should have been fully engaged, I can only apologise. My children Billy, Lila and Scarlett have listened to their father 'banging on about Brexit' for far too long. It would truly delight them if this book marked the beginning of the end of that journey.